Hindu-Buddhist Philosophy *on* Conflict Avoidance *and* Environment Consciousness

Hindu-Buddhist Philosophy *on* Conflict Avoidance *and* Environment Consciousness

SAMVAD—A GLOBAL INITIATIVE (II)

Vivekananda International Foundation
New Delhi

PENTAGON PRESS LLP

Hindu-Buddhist Philosophy on Conflict Avoidance and Environment Consciousness
Samvad—A Global Initiative (II)

ISBN 978-93-86618-96-2

First Published in 2020

Published by
PENTAGON PRESS LLP
206, Peacock Lane, Shahpur Jat,
New Delhi-110049
Phones: 011-64706243, 26491568
Telefax: 011-26490600
email: rajan@pentagonpress.in
website: www.pentagonpress.in

Printed in India By Thomson Press India Ltd.

CONTENTS

ENVIRONMENT CONSCIOUSNESS
FOR A SUSTAINABLE WORLD

ROUND TABLE OF THE SPIRITUAL MASTERS

SUMMATION

INTRODUCTION

1

Welcome Address: Ashin Nyanissara

I would like to extend my warmest greetings to all the religious leaders, brothers and sisters present here at this august gathering with wishes for your physical and mental well-being. It gives me great pleasure today to meet with over a 100 religious leaders from 30 countries. I feel as though I have got a great opportunity to meet my siblings, from a previous life again. It is with this feeling, that we have tried our utmost best to make you comfortable during your stay in Myanmar.

We live in different parts of the world with diversities in faith, culture and life style, we are gathered here today with the unique aim for peace, security and stability of the human world which, in other words, is the common goal of all faiths.

I earnestly hope that all participants will engage in a free exchange of views, ideas and experiences so that this Inter Faith Dialogue can be a resounding success and have an outcome, that is conducive to our efforts to better promote world peace and stability.

Although there is a desire for peace throughout the world, most people are not in a position to experience the peace, security and stability they desire. We are today living in a world of political, racial and religious conflict that results in brutal fighting, killings, chaos and aggression. The root cause of this, I believe, is that the numbers of atheists are increasing day by day, in every part of the world. I have noted with grave concern that 35 per cent of the people in England are atheists; 31 per cent in Japan and 33 per cent in the US. There are a large number of atheists even in the birthplaces of the world's five major religions. It is tragic to see that with the advancement of science and technology, followers of different faiths have become less interested in the teachings of their respective religions, resulting in the failure to observe religious discipline that prevents them from committing evil. This is a most alarming issue which poses the biggest threat to world peace, stability and security.

So, let me remind you that first of all, we the religious leaders need to practice the teachings of our respective religions. What we speak and how we behave must be an example for our followers. Secondly, we need to teach our followers to fully understand the tenets of our respective religions and to follow them accordingly.

Peace-loving political leaders are working hard for world peace through a number of organisations. We, the religious leaders, are also doing our part for achieving the same goal through this world conferences of faiths. We have a common platform for attaining our goal of peace, security and stability. As you are all aware, there are many rivers in the world the Irrawaddy in Myanmar, the Ganges in India, the Yellow river in China, the Mississippi in the US. Despite their different names, they share the common characteristic of purifying and cleansing anyone who takes a dip in them and refreshing his tired soul with a sip of their water. In the same manner, however different we are in terms of the faiths we profess, we have something quite unique in common, which is our firm resolve to make the world peaceful and stable.

I would like to beseech all religious leaders, while accepting the unity in diversity concept, to join hands and make common cause to further strengthen peace, security and stability in the world.

(Dr Ashin Nyanissara is the Most Venerable Sitagu Sayadaw of the Sitagu International Buddhist Academy, Yangon)

2

Welcome Address: NC Vij

IT is a great personal privilege for me to welcome you all in Yangon, the city of Shwe Dagon and the capital of the Golden Land of Myanmar.

The Samvad initiative as we all know was born out of dialogue between the Prime Ministers of India and Japan, finding a new model and vision for a world order based on the spirit of human cooperation, ethical behaviour, universal responsibility and prosperity of all nations based on the foundations of the shared non-conflicting philosophic and civilizational paradigm. Samvad was thus conceived as an ambitious, yet not an unachievable, initiative aiming to shift the paradigm of global discourse on the two critical issues facing humankind of *conflicts* from **Conflict Resolution to Conflict Avoidance** and of *Environment* from Environmental Regulations to Environmental Consciousness.

It is with this aim that the Vivekananda International Foundation (VIF), New Delhi hosted the first Samvad—*Global Hindu-Buddhist Initiative on Conflict Avoidance and Environmental Consciousness* in New Delhi, India in September 2015 in collaboration with The Tokyo Foundation and International Buddhist Confederation (IBC). Over 200 delegates participated in the conference, including the most eminent spiritual leaders of Buddhism, Hinduism and other faiths, eminent thinkers and scholars from all over the world. We were also extremely blessed to have the benediction address by Most Venerable Sitagu Sayadaw Dr Ashin Nyanissara and Param Pujya Sri Sri Ravi Shankar ji, in the august presence of the Hon Prime Minister of India, Shri Narendra Modi, former President of Sri Lanka, Mrs. Chandrika Kumaratunga Bhandaranaike and other distinguished leaders from Bhutan, Nepal, Mongolia and Cambodia. The Hon'ble Prime Minister of Japan also addressed the gathering via video message.

Underlining his commitment to Samvad initiative, the Prime Minister of India also led the delegates after the conference in New Delhi in visiting the Holy city of Bodhgaya and prayed for peace under the Sacred Bodhi Tree at the Mahabodhi temple. In his address, he once again delved on the strength of the shared Hindu Buddhist heritage and Asian values and stated that Hindu philosophy was one of the greatest beneficiaries of advent and teachings of Buddha and his enlightened awakening was enlightenment of Hinduism too. Terming Bodh Gaya as a land with distinctive place in the history of humankind and pilgrimage, he called for developing Bodh Gaya as the spiritual capital and a site of civilisational bond between India and the Buddhist world. He assured all support from the government of India for the same.

A Declaration of Buddhist Religions and Spiritual Leaders also known as 'Bodhgaya Declaration' was read and adopted in Prime Minister Modi's presence which he described as a pioneering document that will show us the way ahead. His message to this august gathering and his continuous support for furthering this initiative is a matter of great strength for us. I will request all to deliberate, suggest and contribute to realise the aspirations articulated in the Declaration and the vision of making Bodhgaya the spiritual capital of the world.

In January 2016, our partners in Japan followed up with a Symposium in 'Shared Values and Democracy in Asia' which was hosted by Nikkei Inc., the Tokyo Foundation, and Vivekananda International Foundation in association with The Japan Foundation and International Buddhist Confederation. The symposium further explored and exchanged informed insights into shared values and democracy in the spirit of fulfilling the promise of the 21st century as an Asian century.

In his video message, the Hon. Prime Minister of India Shri Narendra Modi reiterated the theme of Samvad-I and stated "All Asian civilizations had a common value system that recognizes, accepts, and even celebrates diversity among humans. This is what leads to conflict avoidance, as it is founded on harmony in diversity. Conflict avoidance based on harmonizing the diversity of humans is inherent in Asian democracy as its basic value."

The former Indonesian president Susilo Bambang Yudhoyono and Rev. Kosei Morimoto, Abbot Emeritus of Japan's iconic Todaiji temple delivered the keynote address. In his valedictory address, the Hon. Prime Minister of Japan, Mr Shinzo Abe reminisced about his visit to the Holy city of Varanasi with Prime Minister Modi and attending Ganga Aarti and being dazzled at the bottomless depths of history connecting both ends of Asia. He further elaborated on the inevitability of "twists and turns" in nurturing democratic momentum and stressed on one absolute requirement—namely, being open to others while imparting mutual respect towards differing opinions and points of view.

The unique feature of the Eastern philosophies is that they have provided and continue providing the fulcrum for the ethical and responsible society and motivates us to follow truthful principles of life.

Hence speaking of the environmental consciousness; religion and environment are one and the same for Buddhism and Hinduism. Buddhist practice of *ahimsa* (non violence) and *karuna* (compassion) applies not just to human beings, but to all sentient beings—any living thing that has a mind. Similarly, as per the Upanishads, every sentient being has a grain of the divinity that has created the Universe and hence each creation needs to be respected. Thus we share a sense of universal responsibility for both mankind and nature.

As a soldier I can testify that war is never a permanent solution to any problem and should be avoided as far as possible and the highest priority should be accorded to conflict resolution, or even better—"conflict avoidance".

I am sure the spiritual masters, learned scholars and delegates will engage in frank and honest discussions with an open heart over the next two days. I also hope that they will evolve a consensus on the need for a fresh approach to deal with violence, environmental degradation and take the lead in pursuing the path of sustainable peace, harmony and security.

In this respect we feel so fortunate to have the patronage of Most Venerable Sitagu Sayadaw Dr Ashin Nyanissara, who so graciously and generously offered to host this edition of Samvad at the Sitagu International Buddhist Academy in Yangon in the blessed golden shadow of the great Shwe Dagon Pagoda. It also gives us great joy that His excellency the Governor of the State of Uttar Pradesh, Shri Ram Naik ji is the Chief Guest today. On behalf of the organisers and associates I extend a warm welcome to you, sir.

I would like to mention here, that the Vivekananda International Foundation takes inspiration from Swami Vivekananda's teachings. The modern management concept stems from the notion of 'Practical Vedanta' as preached and propagated by Swami Vivekananda all across the world. Swamiji explained the concept of Vedanta, earlier known only to the Rishis and saints, to the common man in the simplest possible language. Its principles are most relevant in today's context. The society that practices *Practical Vedanta* can conquer both the internal and external worlds peacefully, while avoiding the negative implications of environmental abuse. That is why Swamiji says, *'All differences in this world are of degree, and not of kind, because oneness is the secret of everything.'*

This knowledge emanates from the timeless wisdom as mentioned in the Maha Upanishad '*Vasudhaiva Kutumbakam*', meaning 'the whole world is-one single family'. I hope and pray that our timeless wisdom of peace, compassion and empathy will continue to be our guiding light in our journey on the path of collective prosperity.

(General NC Vij is Former Chief of Indian Army. He was Director VIF from 2014–2017)

3

Narendra Modi

FRIENDS, it is a matter of great honor for me to address this distinguished gathering of religious scholars and thinkers from across the world representing various religions and traditions for Samvad on the theme of Dialogue for Peace, Harmony and Security.

It is a matter of great satisfaction that over the last two years SAMVAD has grown from strength to strength. It has brought together diverse scholars and thinkers from all over the world to reflect on challenges that confront humanity today.

Societies across the world are facing several questions today:

1. How to avoid conflict?
2. How to address the global challenges like climate change?
3. What lessons do Asian values and democracies hold for the world?
4. How to live with peace and harmony and secure our lives?

All these questions are not only timeless and deeply philosophical, they are also relevant to our contemporary world. It is only natural that the search for answers be led by humanities longest traditions of thought, rooted in various religions, civilisations and multiple streams of spirituality.

Friends, I am a product of the ancient Indian tradition that humbly believes in dialogue on difficult issues. The ancient Indian concept of Tarkshastra is founded on dialogue and debate as the model for exchange of views and avoidance of conflicts.

In Indian Mythology, Krishna killed Kansa and Prince Siddhartha who later became Lord Buddha saved a dog hurt by an arrow shot by his brother.

Also, Lord Rama obeyed his father while Bhakta Prahalad disobeyed his father. On the surface this may appear contradictory but the purpose of each action was to uphold Dharma which has sustained Indians from ancient to modern times. It is only through deep and prolonged dialogue Samvad that we may discover hidden synergies and resolve contradictions.

Samvad is also the only way to cut through deep rooted religious stereotypes and prejudices that often arise due to misconceptions and divide communities across the world and saw seeds of conflicts between nations and societies.

Friends, the Hindu-Buddhist philosophies also see nature and its entire creation as one whole. They advocate living in harmony with nature.

If man does not nurture nature, then nature reacts in the form of climate change. Environmental laws and regulations while essential in any modern society, effer only an inferior protection to nature. What is needed is harmonious environmental consciousness. Man must relate to nature. Man must revere nature not merely consider it as resource to be exploited.

Friends, Asia the world's most populous geography is amazingly complex and wonderfully varied. It is also home to incredible diversity of spiritual and philosophical traditions. As the interconnected and interdependent world of 21st century battles a number of global challenges from terrorism to climate change. I am confident that the solutions will be found through Asia's oldest traditions of dialogue and debate.

My best wishes are with you, as you discuss, deliberate and debate many issues both practical and philosophical over these two days. I would also like to convey my heartiest congratulations to Sitagu International Buddhist Academy, Myanmar Institute of Strategic and International studies, Vivekananda International Foundation, The Japan Foundation and Government of Myanmar for organising this edition of Samvad.

(Mr Narendra Modi is the Hon'ble Prime Minister of India)

4

Shinzo Abe

GOOD morning, I am Shinzo Abe. First I would like to extend my heartfelt congratulation to "*Samvad – II: Dialogue for Peace, Harmony and Security*" in Yangon. In Asia, people have pursued various thoughts and religions from ancient times. While different paths were followed by Buddhism, Hinduism, Confucianism or Islam, we all pursued some form of "Law" or "Dharma" and lived together. "May all living beings be happy." This famous quote from Buddha, shows the spirits of tolerance and compassion that appeal coexistence of all lives. This belief in tolerance flows from the source to the rivers of Asian values, and has supported diversity in Asia. It is because of such ideas that "democracy," which was born in Europe, took root and flourished here in Asia. In Myanmar in order to realize people's hope, under the "21st century Panglong Union Peace Conference", different ethnic groups are continuing dialogue on peace. State Counselor Daw Aung San Suu Kyi said, "We can find similarities despite our differences, and that we can identify common ground through peaceful negotiation." As a friend of the people of Myanmar, Japan is ready to support such aspiration. Meanwhile, the spirit of tolerance is facing challenges today. Terrorism and violent extremism is expending and trying to deny the existence of "others" and to paint our world in a single color. Such attempts should not be tolerated. In Asia, we must let flowers of all different colors bloom in harmony. Finally, "freedom" which brings tolerance and diversity is the source of growth and creativity. Asia's significant development that we enjoy today is based on freedoms of thought, speech and commerce that those before us have carefully nurtured. Free, open, diverse and tolerant Asia; Asia where nobody is excluded; Asia, where sustainable growth is realized. These are the values that Japan would like to realize under the "Free and Open Indo-Pacific Strategy." I sincerely hope for diverse and faithful discussions in the spirit of tolerance during this seminar.

(Mr Shinzo Abe is the Hon'ble Prime Minister of Japan)

5

BENEDICTION: SWAMI AVDESHANAND GIRI

Om vishwani deva, savitar duritani parasuva, yad bhadram tannay asuva.
Om shanti, shanti, shanti hi. Om.

I bless the gathering on behalf of the Hindu Dharma Acharya Sabha, comprising of the various traditions of Hindu *Dharma*. I am happy to be present on this occasion, at Sitagu Institute in the land committed to *Dharma.* I welcome the various religious leaders representing different religions, other leaders, the governor of Gujarat and thank the organisers of this function.

Today wherever we look we find insecurity, fear and conflict all over the world. Not only at the global level, but at the individual level also there is disturbance, stress and insecurity. In this scenario, this dialogue will bring great blessings on humanity and the world per se.

There is a saying in our tradition, '*Vaade vaade jayate tattvabodhaha*'. The more you discuss, the more you engage in dialogue, the better you discover the truth. That being the case, when humanity is looking for long-lasting peace, long-lasting fullness, long-lasting happiness, I am sure this dialogue will provide a way out for humanity and bestow blessings on everyone.

Our scriptures give quite a simple definition of *Dharma* i.e. *Atmanaha pratikulani paresham na samacharet.* What gives me pain, what gives me insecurity, unhappiness and disturbs me, I do not do that unto others. When this vision or commitment is imbibed into one's daily life, there will be peace in the world.

According to our scriptures and culture, everything on this Earth, living creatures, sentient and insentient beings, plants and animals as well as other natural elements, are not only meant for our consumption (*bhoga*), we also must contribute to creation. *Ten taktyen bhunjitaha*, this *vaakya* from the *vedas* means that we should first contribute to creation and then become a consumer. There are words like *tyaaga* which mean that you need to give up something. All environmental problems such as global warming and natural disasters are caused primarily, because we look upon the world as something to be consumed, not to be respected. Our tradition, our *dharma* teaches us to worship creation which is not different from the manifestation of the Lord himself.

Hindu leaders begin every endeavour by praying for all living creatures. The teachings of our scriptures are the inspiration behind this prayer i.e. '*Vasudhaiva kutumbakam*' which means that all of creation, including ourselves, is nothing but the expression and manifestation of the Lord. Therefore, all living creatures are but our brothers and sisters. We look upon creation as one family. That being the case we must protect the rights, needs, requirements of all creatures. Therefore, Indian culture has been singing songs of world peace from day one and can thus be a torchbearer for bringing about peace.

When an individual seeks total peace and happiness, or what we call *moksha*, our scriptures and traditions teach us, that even in that pursuit, we should always respect other traditions, other peoples' faith and others' pursuit of total peace as well. Censuring, belittling or looking down on other religions should not be done. If one does it, it implies disrespect for one's own religion. Therefore, we need to respect all religious and cultural traditions.

There are several conflicts, problems and wars in the world, of which 75 to 80% of global conflicts in the last century as stated during the Millennium Peace Summit, at Harvard University, are caused by religious beliefs. Thus most of the conflicts were religion based. Though most religions advocate and talk about peace, but they look down upon other religions, or do not accept other religions. Religious leaders should engage in constant dialogue, to resolve conflicts and respect one another. There are infinite ways in which we can build a better world for the next generation. Just to aggressively pursue the path of conversion, for expanding our religions is nothing but a kind of *hinsa* or violence.

I am touched by the pure environment of this country. It is a good beginning to bring about stability and peace in this world. On behalf of the Hindu Dharma Acharya Sabha, I congratulate and bless the organisers of this dialogue. It is a historical meeting and I'm sure it will be a good beginning for creating a stable and peaceful world.

According to our tradition and *vedas* the Lord is nothing but the embodiment of fullness, happiness, and that is what every individual aspires to attain. We achieve this fullness, completeness and happiness through our prayers, when we surrender to the Lord. With this prayer, I invoke the blessings of the Lord.

Om purnamadah purnamidam purnaat purnamudachyate.
Purnasya purnamaadaya purnameva vashishyate.
Om shaantihi, shaantihi, shaantihi.

May there be fullness and happiness all around.

(Swami Avdeshanand Giri is Acharya Mahamandeleshwar of Juna Akhara and Head, Hindu Dharma Acharya Sabha, India)

6

U Aung Thein Nyunt

IT is a great pleasure and privilege for me to convey my sincere congratulations to the Samvad II: Dialogue for Peace Harmony and Security-a global Initiative for Peace and Environment Consciousness, jointly organised by Vivekananda International Foundation (VIF), New Delhi, India; Sitagu International Buddhist Academy (SIBA), Yangon; The Japan Foundation, and with collaboration of Myanmar Institute of Strategic and International Studies (MISIS), Yangon on August 5th, 6th 2017 at Sitagu International Buddhist Academy (SIBA), Yangon.

It also gives me a great pleasure and honour to extend my warm greetings and best wishes to the organisers of the conference and also to give deep respect and felicitation to all esteemed participants from different fields of various countries and organisation for taking part in this august assembly to deliberate on the growing demand of Peace and Environment sustainability. I focus attention on the importance of conflict avoidance, as I am an Union Minister for religious affairs and culture. As we know for million people around the world, there religious faith is what helps them make sense of their lives, many people find that religion gives meaning to their lives. They gain strength from it by reading the holy books of their religion or by praying or by meditating or by joining other believers to worship or by giving help to those are in need and in these religious faith there may also be more to believe than what we can see and touch. There may also be something holy that is greater than us. Therefore, there are, the six main religions of the World along with many new religious sects that have also come into existence through the past.

Every religion teaches us the best of best in world by numerous ways, one—by showing us a good and bigger way of life by teaching us theory, and the other is towards bringing theory into practice.

Consequently, civilised cultural human societies manifest themselves on the surface of the globe, except for some remarkable religious conflicts of the past which were unresponsive to the mood of inhabitants collected in related religion.

Responsible religious leaders were also able to lead their followers to righteous and virtuous ways of living and thus in most part of the world we have blessed and peaceful habitats to live in.

But, through the technology of modern civilisation, modern populations have to face a great deal of predicaments. There is a big gap in modern life between provision and priorities. The religious faith they have, may be of immense help to them, but they neglect their religious teaching.

They never think that religion teaches how to live a peaceful and proper life and this is related to the success and prosperity of their lives. Simultaneously some of the responsible religionists do not take interest in imparting knowledge of the journey and teachings shown by their respective religions and some even lead their followers towards the wrong way by imparting an insincere doctrine in the name of religion. In this way most of the faithful stay aloof from their religious centres, and they gradually come to disbelieve their religions. As a result, the population of, hethens, agnostics, pagans, infidels, barbarians, becomes greater than ever in numbers.

At present, we of all the diverse religions, have to make a duress effort to save this unwelcome situation and reform our roots for the sustainability of the faithful. First, we all the religious leaders have to demonstrate compassionately to them that genuine teachings and implementation of them have a profound and beneficial effect. And then, that is how we have to lead them and equip them with the fundamental principles of morality.

The Buddha taught the following ten that become the Doctrine—

"Decrease:

1. Being void of morality and virtue
2. Being void of a steadfast face
3. Having limited knowledge
4. Being stubborn and disobedient

5. Having evil companions
6. Being Indolent and ignorant
7. Being heedless and forgetful
8. Being deceitful and un-principled
9. Earning difficult and Insufficient livelihood
10. being foolish and stupid."

Moreover, the Buddha also taught the following:

- No preaching in detail
- No teaching in detail
- No loud recitation

According to the above teaching of the Buddha, it is very easy to understand that if we all do not pay deep regard to them—the teachings & ideas—Religion will completely disappear from this Earth. The World will unquestionably be devastated. The creation of infidels will lead to the whole World being unbalanced and unhinged by these self-destructive and obstructive elements, who are the major hinderance to peace. Before these elements become greater in number, all the religious leaders should put a laborious effort into working together, in unison for imparting genuine religious teachings to the followers, exemplifying our own righteous and virtuous way of life. May all the religious teachers be united on the same platform for this.

(Mr Thura U Aung Ko is Union Minister for Religious & Cultural Affairs, Govt of Myanmar)

7

Ram Naik

I am extremely privileged to have the honour of being invited to this very important conference and to speak before this august assembly of spiritual masters, eminent thinkers and scholars. It is not for me to speak much in front of such accomplished and revered masters, except to feel blessed and perhaps count the merits of my good karma to be in this company, especially in the land of sacred ShweDagon.

The first leg of this conference, titled 'Samvad', was held on September 3-4, 2015 in New Delhi. It was an extremely insightful and watershed event that aimed to bring about a paradigm shift in the hitherto prevalent global discourse on the themes of 'Conflict Avoidance' and 'Environmental Consciousness'.

It is here on this very soil of Myanmar that the last Buddhist Council was convened from 1954 to 1956 in keeping with the tradition of the first four councils of ancient India. It is therefore more than apt that Myanmar is hosting the second leg of this global initiative 'Samvad II: Dialogue for Peace, Harmony & Security'. It is a symbolic continuation of our shared historical, cultural and spiritual heritage. We share our prayers, our religion, our sorrow and the graves of the last Mughal Emperor Bahadur Shah Zafar in Yangon and the King Thibaw in Ratnagiri in India, both exiled by British colonial rulers. Lokmanya Bal Gangadhar Tilak, 'Father of Indian unrest'—so described by the British rulers—who declared that "Independence is my birth right and I will have it" was jailed in Mandela where he wrote the historical treatise *Geeta-Rahasya*, which is a treatise on the *Bhagwad Geeta*. It was Subhash Chandra Bose who thundered in the historic City Hall: "Give me your blood and I will give you the freedom."

The great sacred Pagoda of ShweDagon is the living symbol of our shared cultural and religious traditions. Besides the holy relics of Gautam Buddha, the sacred Pagoda also celebrates Lord Brahma, who is worshipped by both the Hindus and Buddhists, as the creator and protector of all seven realms.

Early Indian thinker and philosopher had nearly 5000 years ago in the Vedic period declared their love for entire humanity in these words which I quote:

> अयं निजः परोवेति गणनां लघुचेतसाम्,
> उदार चरितानां तु वसुधैव कुटुम्बकम् ।
>
> *Only narrow minded people think this is mine and that is yours. For large hearted people, the entire world is like one family*

The Indian Parliament has engraved this quotation on its walls as its motto.

To us Indians, Myanmar is Brahm Desh, the land of Brahma. As many as 37 deities in Myanmarese culture are common to the Hindus. *YamaZatdaw* is Myanmar's adaption of the Indian epic *Ramayana.* We are bound together not only by our deities, but also by our destinies, by our shared cosmology and the realms of after life.

In modern times, this indelible bond between our two countries has been further strengthened by an extensive and effortless people to people connect. Right from our former first lady Ms Usha Narayanan to prominent personalities in films, politics and business, the people of Myanmar have revered this land as their second home. Here I need to name the Padma Bhushan awardee Shri S.N.Goenka, a renowned Burmese-Indian teacher of Vipassana meditation. Also known as 'the man who taught the world to meditate in the Burmese forest tradition', Shri Goenka laid the foundation of the Global Vipassana Pagoda in Mumbai as a tribute to his master Sayagyi U Ba Khin, who wanted to pay back India, the land of origin of Vipassana. His teachings were notable for emphasising that the Buddha's path to liberation was non-sectarian, universal and scientific in character. Such is the strength of our deeply inter-woven heritage that today, this tradition of meditation is being practiced in over 94 countries. It will not be wrong to say that by the gift of meditation and yoga, Asia has persuaded the world to take a pause and look within. You will be surprised to know that the Pagoda in Mumbai is located at Gorai which has been part of my parliamentary constituency North Mumbai. Moreover Vipassana Guru's son Shri Murarilal Goenka and myself reside in the same building, Lakshachandi, in Mumbai.

The rising attraction of the Eastern philosophies in the West is a globally acknowledged reality. The holistic nature of these philosophies ingrained in sustainable societal good while empowering the human individual, has attracted people across the world. Hinduism and Buddhism are the two most ancient belief systems in the world and together they have given rise to a syncretic society in the subcontinent, that is inherently peace loving and harmonious. Here, I am using the word harmonious for a reason. 'Tolerance' implies acceptance of different ways, whereas harmony connotes essential co-existence, stemming from the deep rooted belief that differences are superficial, and that every path leads us all to the same ultimate truth—which the Buddhists call 'Nirvana', while the Hindus refer to it as 'Moksha'. Anyone who realises this, would agree that our conflicts have emanated from our limited understanding of world, negating the essential unity of all sentient beings.

Both Hindu and Buddhist philosophies have a rich tradition of dialectics; a democratic process of debate based on logic and reasoning that underlines acceptance and divergence, based on mutual understanding and respect. This provided a strong cultural base for the society's development and acceptance of diversity. Appropriately titled 'Samvad', a derivative of the Sanskrit word '*Samvaadam*' (meaning 'Dialogue'), the speakers at the conference will urge open and truthful global dialogue on avoiding conflict and nurturing environmental consciousness. A candid and healthy discussion among all stakeholders on a continuous basis, is the time tested key to avoid chaos and turbulence.

The 'Delhi Samvad Conference' was an endeavour to transform the meet into a new movement—a global intellectual and civilisational movement to create deep awareness and to spread and advocate three themes in global discourse, namely:

- From curative conflict resolution to preventive conflict avoidance
- From state environmental regulation to mass ecological consciousness
- From the dialogue-evasive ideology to dialogue-friendly philosophy.

This conference was intended to initiate the process by holding a series of conferences first in Asian nations, to carry and deepen the agenda and later in other places.

Hindu and Buddhist traditions have compatible views on environmental issues. Buddhism is very clear in its teaching that often the cause of wrong doing is ignorance rather than wickedness or sin. The natural corollary of this, in the context of the environment, is the need for environmental education. The *'Aarya-ashtaangika Marg'* or the noble eight fold path stresses on 'right' thought, vision, action and livelihood, to name a few, which implies protecting and preserving Mother Earth and her children. Just to cite an example, King Asoka's Fifth Pillar Edict listing the various species of wild animals under protection, is one of the earliest recorded instances, of a specific governmental policy of conservation. It is equally remarkable that people in Vedic times regarded nature and environment in holistic manner and refrained from such activities that could harm *'panchamaahaabhoota'*—the five basic sacred elements. These elements are nothing but Earth, Water, Fire, Wind and Sky, and all are nature's bounties.

When the world is struggling to find the ways and means to ensure a clean environment, our syncretic way of nurturing an environmental consciousness is replete with perspectives on a long term sustainable future for all.

For peace and security to flourish, it is essential for Eastern philosophies to come together. Today, when the world is witnessing increasing levels of polarisation in conflict situations, spiritual masters, non-conflicting philosophies and democratic societies must work together to preserve and promote non-conflicting traditions and democratic values.

The resurgence of Asia on global panorama imposes greater responsibility on Asian countries for taking the lead in fostering meaningful dialogue for conflict avoidance and preserving and promoting the environmental culture practiced by our ancestors. For that to happen, Eastern philosophies need to seek greater convergence and promote their shared spiritual heritage. In present times, it is all the more important to imbibe Buddha's cardinal message of *Appo Deepo Bhava*—'be your own light', to appreciate the Upanishadic vision of *Sarvam Khalvidm Bramhasmi*, meaning 'matter and spirit are non-different from the Supreme Consciousness'.

(Mr Ram Naik is Governor of Uttar Pradesh, India)

8

Aung San Suu Kyi

TODAY, it takes a great pleasure and honour for me to attend the opening ceremony of **Samvad II: Dialogue for Peace, Harmony and Security—A Global Initiative for Conflict Avoidance and Environment Consciousness,** jointly organized by the Vivekananda International Foundation(VIF, New Delhi), Sitagu International Buddhist Academy (SIBA, Yangon) and the Japan Foundation in close collaboration with Myanmar Institute of Strategic and International Studies (MISIS, Yangon) on August 5-6, 2017 at Sitagu International Buddhist Academy (SIBA),Yangon. I would like to extend my sincere congratulations and goodwill to the organizers of this conference and also to pay deep respect and congratulate all the participants from different faiths of various countries and organizations for taking part in this august assembly.

In this esteemed assembly we all are going to deliberate on the growing demand for peace building and environmental sustainability—A Global Initiative for Conflict Avoidance and Environment Consciousness. As I am a State Counsellor and Union Minister for Foreign Affairs of Myanmar Government, may I emphasize the importance of **"Conflict Avoidance" which is the major issue for development of Environment Consciousness.**

Through the ages of Myanmar history there has been no remarkable discrimination against races and religion, majority and minority; in the same way individual right of all indigenous people in Myanmar has also not been limited nor resistricted. Myanmar government always tries to build a happy and peaceful human society for all of the Myanmar citizens.

According to the section Nos. 34, 348, and 363 of the Constitution of the Union of Myanmar, it is distinctly prescribed that:—**"Every citizen is equally entitled to freedom of conscience and the right to freely confess and**

practise religion subject to public order, morality or health and to the other provisions of this Constitution." Besides, **"There is no discrimination against race and religion, social standards, culture, gender among the Myanmar citizens; the Union may assist and protect the religions it recognizes to its utmost."**

In section No.153 (a) and 295-to-298 of the Criminal Law it is also advocated that "those who attempt to incite racial and religious hatred and animosity among diverse group of Myanmar people by any verbal or correspondence or gesture or any other distinctive manner and behaviour shall be taken into legal action."

Besides, a religion must not maltreat and harm other religions by means of bodily or verbal actions; in order not to distress, jeopardize and defame every religious faith, the equal rights and protection are given for the benefit of every religious follower.

For safeguarding the right of indigenous languages and literature, arts and culture, custom and tradition, race and religion and historical heritages around the country **"The Law to Safeguard and Protect the Rights of National Races"** was enacted by Pyi Htaungsu Hluttaw in 2015.

The Ministry of Religious Affairs and Culture organized the very first Interfaith Dialogue at the uppermost level from different four major religions of Myanmar in 2008. Up to June 2012 the Interfaith Dialogue Group of Central Level had been reorganized for 3 times in 2008, 2010 and 2012. Later, the Central Group by themselves tried to organize different levels of group in 11 States and Divisions including District levels, Township levels, Ward and Village-tract levels. In these groups Buddhist monks as well as lay-persons from different major religions participate in these groups, discharging their respective duties to achieve the following prescribed aims and objectives:

(1) To build the unity of diverse religions;
(2) To prevent and protect from arising religious crisis;
(3) To settle down the situation of crisis;
(4) To help the needy people who suffer different sorts of disasters and to be rehabilitate them;
(5) To have a chance of free confessions in their respective religions;
(6) To mutually understand and pay respect one another in view of religious faith;
(7) To impart genuine teachings of religions to the respective followers;

(8) To build a peaceful and prosperous human society based on the ethics of common platform **"Unity in Diversity"**.

Some of religious and ethnic conflicts and dissensions among diverse religious faiths and ethnic groups occurred in our country are aroused and inflamed by those who do not want stability and peace of the country for some reasons, inciting to hate-speech among the people rooted in racial and religious hatred and animosity.

As suggested by the Union Minister for Religious Affairs and Culture, the central members of the Interfaith Dialogue drafted **a Bill for Protection against Hate-Speech** in May 2016 for working on the improvement of unity and peace among diverse religious faiths. The Ministry revised the Bill with the recommendation of the Union Office of Attorney-General for two times in 2016 and put forward the Revised Bill to the President's Office for approval. This Bill was forwarded to **the Committee for Security, Stability, Law-abiding** for taking a further necessary action as instructed by the President's Office. Now this Bill is under scrutinization through different legislative organizations.

All the above are the preventive measures against religious and racial conflicts for our own country. In order to build a global conflict avoidance architecture, in a Buddhist point of view, we all have to pay deep attention to human mind. The Buddha taught that:

> "All mental phenomena have mind as their fore-runner; they have mind as their chief; they are mind-made. If one speaks or acts with an evil mind suffering and sorrow follows him just a wheel follows the foot-print of the ox that draws the cart. If one speaks or acts with pure mind, peace and happiness follows him like a shadow that never leaves him. (Dham,1,2)".

Here is my humble suggestion for tackling "Conflict Avoidance": all religious leaders of the world have to impart the knowledge of genuine noble teachings being embedded in every world religion to their respective followers—up to the grassroots levels, for living a moral way of life, for keeping their minds on the positive results, and for cultivating purity of their mind. All the sacred scriptures call for peace and amity, harmony and sympathy. All great founders of all religions have emphasized it with virtues of tolerance and non-violence. Having discovered the blissful peace within overselves, we should make an arduous attempt to establish community peace, regional peace and global peace.

It is very important for all of us to impart the intrinsic noble teachings of our respective religions to our followers up to grassroots level and to make them practise these teachings accordingly.

- May the balanced mind make unbalanced world balanced!
- May all conflicts and animosity be ceased!
- May peace and harmony prevail everywhere!

(Daw Aung San Suu Kyi is State Counsellor and the Union Minister for Foreign Affairs, Republic of the Union of Myanmar)

Evolving A Non-Conflicting Philosophical Paradigm for Conflict Avoidance, Peace & Harmony

1

S Gurumurthy

Why Samvad?

WHEN Samvad was thought of, why was it thought of? It was thought of because the world has been drawn into a complex vortex of conflicts from where it's not finding any way for retrieval. It is as if people have lost hope that there could be peace and harmony. The world seems to be preparing more for an enduring conflict today. Not many wager for peace. This is the situation to which we have come. It is no more a fight between nations, but it has become a fight between people—within nations and outside. The worst thing that can happen to a society is not when two nations are fighting, but when people fight among themselves.

When two nations fight, it is war, when peoples fight, it is anarchy. War is not abnormal at all. It is normal for nations to fight and wage war with one another. But, when people are fighting, they are killing each other, it is anarchy. Nations fight over territories and power. Religions are supposed to prevent wars even between nations. But when religions themselves fight, the situation is dangerous. This is what human history particularly in the Abrahamic world has taught us. The killing not just takes place between two religions or nations driven by different religions, but it is also within a single religion. When Samuel Huntington spoke of civilisational clashes, he spoke of clashes between religiously-driven civilisations. While Francis Fukuyama prognosticated end of conflicts, Huntington forecast a reinstatement of medieval barbarism. As the 21st century began, it was Huntington who seems to be proven right, and not Fukuyama.

Need Philosophers to Handle Ideology-Generated Conflicts

Is this where we have come to in the last 20-25 years? Most of the religious conflicts are rooted within or between exclusive belief systems, or between exclusive religions and others who are not exclusive. The conflicts have been theologically conceptualised and generated, nurtured, sustained and activated by religious and political activists. These are prompted or promoted by some states. Other states have not contained or prevented them. Being not a state-originated and states vs states conflict, they cannot be handled by just political systems or political institutions, nor can the media, which function on contemporary paradigms or public discourse, which reflects these institutions, stop it or help to contain it. Competitive and sensational media particularly can only fuel it and cannot quench it nor suggest a solution for it. It is beyond the capacity of liberals and intellectuals who operate on contemporary and contextual paradigms like political institutions and media, to deal with them. Why can contemporary institutions not handle them?

Institutions and ideas which are products of contextual compulsions have limited shelf life and lack the durability, while religions seem to have unlimited shelf-life and durability. Even such far-reaching and earth-shaking ideas like socialism and globalisation have weakened and fatigued in less than a quarter century. Even its predecessors did not have the durability that the values and traditions inherited from thousands of years by different societies and nations, particularly outside the Abrahamic societies, have demonstrated. The contemporary ideas and institutions of the last 200 years have shown increasingly decreasing shelf life. For example, the powerful wave of colonialism lasted for 200 years. Its heir, mercantile capitalism lasted for 100 years. Its competitor communism lasted for 50 years and the baby of capitalism, globalisation has fatigued in just 25 years. Their increasingly less and less duration is because they are not driven by contemporary, contextual and fashionable ideas.

All contemporary institutions, which are driven by less and less durable ideas, are witness to conflicts generated by ideologies and were focussed on solutions after allowing such conflicts-generated ideologies to play out. It requires a philosophy and different leaders—philosophers—who live above the contemporary political fog and above what triggers the people to conflict, to initiate the process of conflict avoidance transcending the present. That is why we thought of approaching and involving the spiritual and religious philosophers to help devise conflict avoidance ideas and models for the contemporary institutions so as to avoid ideology-generated conflict. Samvad is the confluence of the religious philosophers, as distinct from religious ideologues, along with the support of contemporary geo-political states and institutions and public intellectuals in developing conflict avoidance models. Samvad seeks to go to the root of the conflicts—the centrifugal religious ideologies that generate the conflict—to deal with them, and not merely stop at conflict resolution which allows the centrifugal ideologies to generate the conflicts.

Tradition and Religion Vs Modernity and Liberalism—The Conflicting Dualism of Contemporary World

SAMVAD initiative is probably the first initiative in "modern world", to approach the philosophic, religious people and spiritualists for solution that the secular domain seems unable to offer. Modernity unmistakably went wrong by virtually rejecting religion. In the last 100-150 years, it has become fashionable to say "I am not a very traditional or religious man", and equally fashionable to say "I am modern", meaning anti-tradition and anti-religion. Modernity and liberalism joined to brand both traditions and religion and anti-modern and liberal. As a result many of them, most intellectuals, liberals and modernists—be it politicians, intellectuals or academics—live a dual life—religious within and modern outside. This is also one of the basic reasons for conflict between the traditional and the modern—with traditions being owned by religion and rejected by modernity. Even non-religious traditions are branded as religious and orphaned in the modern world. This intellectual, academic, and political dualism—particularly in religiously and spiritually sensitive nations mostly in Asia—has distanced the public discourse from people who believe in tradition and religion. This is also the main reason for propensity for conflicts in the modern world.

Anyway, modernity has not been able to undermine, much less do away with religion. Modernity has delegitimised religion in the public domain, and driven it into private domain. The West could manage to do it because its society was largely Christian, not multireligious. The privatisation of religion, coupled with the Western notion of modernity which delegitimises tradition and religion even in private domain, is the main reason for the rise of religion-driven conflicts in religiously sensitive geographies. In such religiously sensitive geographies, modernity is a false exterior, the true interior being religion. You can survey any society, and find that majority of people believe in religion. In a country like India, 98% of people believe in religion and almost all believe in astrology! Modernity does not seem to understand the power of religion. If religion holds sway over people, the state—particularly a democratic state—cannot ask people to disown their religion in the name of modernity and liberalism in public discourse centred on mono-religious Western experiences, making it fashionable to undermine religion and tradition. This one-size-fits-all west-centric economic model leading to one-size-fits-all cultural model of the West is one of the reasons for conflicts in the modern world.

Ideological Religions and Philosophic Religions

Religion, being perhaps the most powerful influence over humans, cannot be ignored or trivialised. Religions have to be involved and made stakeholders through dialogue. Even if conflicts are caused by religious ideologies. The answer to such conflicts is to promote and ideate religious philosophies for countering religious ideologies. But is the involvement of religious and spiritual people capable of delivering this? We thought that if religion was the source of conflict it must also be involved for solution—and in any event we need to involve them in a dialogue. If we can involve terrorists produced by ideological religions in dialogue and talks for peace, could there not be a dialogue among all religious people to avoid conflicts among them and help the modern world to reduce and contain conflicts—at least religious conflicts? Dialogue among religions is necessary even to temper and moderate religions towards one another and also to mediate between modernity and religions and traditions. For strategising the involvement and engagement of the religious people in dialogue, we need to understand the difference between ideology and philosophy to understand the difference between ideological religions and philosophic religions.

It was the former US President Bill Clinton who spoke of the difference between ideology and philosophy. He said philosophy is open to dialogue, but ideology is not. Because ideology presumes itself to be right and others wrong, whereas philosophy presumes there can be another view point. Philosophy is inclusive, ideology is not. This huge difference between ideology and philosophy permeates as difference between ideological religions and philosophic religions. Ideological religions claim to be the only true religions, but philosophic religions do not. It is easier to engage philosophic religions in dialogue as like philosophies, they are open to the other view point, but not ideological religions. Ideological religions which claim their texts and beliefs are inerrant, do not easily lend themselves to dialogue. But in the contemporary world where there is a huge voluntary mix and interaction of people of all nations and religions, as never before in history, no one idea can claim to be eternally inerrant, particularly if that idea is likely to have an impact on those who do not adhere to it. Ideological religions not only presume their texts to be inerrant and its views and beliefs as the only truth, but they also view all others are fake, denying them not only legitimacy but even the right to exist. And that allows no scope for dialogue or debate with those who hold another view. Philosophic religions presume their views are right, but concede that there may be other legitimate views as well. This allows and opens scope for dialogue. In contemporary times when the world is highly interconnected by migration, communication, and trade, no religion can claim to be the only true repository of wisdom, as Swami Vivekananda cautioned them over 100 years ago at the World Parliament of Religions. Saying so, an ideological religion cannot reject all other views as fake if it has to take part in global affairs, unless it chooses to be a cult, cut off from the rest of the world.

Samvad, a sanskrit word, means dialogue. Samvad is an effort to rope in even the ideas that shun dialogue into dialogue. Samvad therefore approaches and involves all religious and spiritual people—whether they belong to the ideological group or philosophic group. After considerable contemplation, Samvad conceptualised the idea of involving religious personalities in the dialogue. There were two reasons why Samvad saw the need to involve religious and spiritual personalities. Religion has become one of the biggest triggers for conflict today. The very source which is supposed to yield peace has become the source of anger, hate, conflict, and violence. Religious violence is today a global threat. We in Samvad, thought it is necessary to involve the very actors from the discipline which is the reason for conflict and seek solutions from the very source where this hate emerges from. That is why SAMVAD focusses on involving religious and spiritual people. This has been our understanding of the role of religions in conflict avoidance dialogue. And for that purpose we do analyse the religions. All religious people, spiritual people, expound our philosophy. While all religious people should study other religious scripts with an open mind, the ideological religious people should study philosophic religions.

In fact, the ancient Hindu and Buddhist traditions had devised a scientific model for dialogue among religions—the *Tarka Shastra* which is common science for Hinduism and Buddhism. The *Tarka Shastra* postulates dialogue among persons who are well versed not only in their religion but also in the religion with whose exponent they seek a dialogue with. That is, if one wants to comment on the other religion, one must first study that religion, then criticise that religion if one sees points to criticise, and then one must allow the other person to criticise one's own religion. The right to mutual criticism is the essence of *Tarka Shastra*. And in dialogue, each religion must have the right to examine the other religion and its fundamentals. This is particularly important as, unlike the philosophic religions which confine their appeal to their own followers, the ideological religions claim right to tread beyond their domain and brand adherents of other religions as *Kafir* or Heathen and set rules as to how they would deal with such non-adherents. This is the source of religiously driven conflicts today, both within the ideological religions and in their relation with other religions whether—ideological or philosophic. No religion can claim or should be allowed to claim its fundamentals that affect its non-adherents, as inerrant and the only truth.

Dialogue Among Religions—Must for Avoiding Conflict Among Religions and Nations

It means there is need to discuss the fundamentals of religions if conflicts are to be avoided. No religion can say its fundamentals are only true and right and, on that basis, judge the other person's religion as wrong therefore calling for him to be converted to their faith because it is the only true faith. Every religion's fundamentals need to be examined through open and transparent dialogue where the dialoguing faiths voluntarily allow their fundamentals to be questioned and criticised by one another. The criticism of the other view point is known as *Purva Paksha* which is the very foundation of *Tarka Shastra*. The contemporary version of the ancient *Tarka Shastra* has been expounded by Hans Kung, a celebrated Catholic Theologian, who advised the German Church on the Vatican Council II in 1965. Despite being a well-known theologian from the stable of an ideological religion which would not allow its fundamentals to be questioned, he suggested a philosophic model for dialogue for peace and harmony among religions, similar to the rules of *Tarka Shastra*. The Hans Kung formula for dialogue among religions rests on three limbs, namely,

- One: there cannot be peace between nations, unless there is peace between religions.

- Two: there cannot be peace between religions unless there is dialogue among religions.
- Three: there cannot be dialogue among religions unless the fundamentals of each religion are allowed to be investigated by the other religion.

For initiating a dialogue whose object is peace among religions and nations, the most critical element is the last limb. One, the fundamentals are of two kinds. Fundamentals that affect only the adherents of a religion and the fundamentals that affect those who are not its adherents. One cannot have a dialogue unless one allows fundamentals affecting non-adherents to be examined. Today in the name of political correctness the examination of fundamentals of a religions is barred at the threshold. If the fundamentals of an ideological religion that lay rules for its non-adherents is examined in the public domain, one need not say the ideological religious person is wrong, because, by the very force of the disciplined dialogue, he will realise he's wrong. That is the beauty of dialogue founded on the principles of *Tarka Shastra* and *Purva Paksha* incorporated in the Hindu-Buddhist traditions. *Purva Paksha* makes an adherent of ideological religion realise where he's at fault without being told he is at fault. That is what SAMVAD intends to do.

The Discipline of Dialogue

Tarka Shastra is founded not on arguments but on logic and high discipline. Absence of hate and anger are the very basis of disciplined dialogue among enlightened persons of two religions. The dialogue is carried out in a logical and mutually respectable manner, without anger or hate. Dialogue is distinct from debate. Debate leads to ego and results in discord even if one wins at the end. Dialogue results in harmony even if the end result is disagreement. The finest example of dialogue of high discipline in Hindu philosophy was the one that took place between Adi Shankara and Mandalamishra. Adi Shankara was the exponent of the *Advaita*—non-dualist philosophy which has the potential to be the common basis for all faiths and religions, whether monotheistic or polytheistic. *Advaita* means that which is not dual, that is the truth is one only. Sankara's *Advaita* recognises the role of rituals, but limits its legitimacy to only as a means to disciplining the body and mind and does not consider rituals as the end in itself. Sankara was asserting the non-dualistic interpretation of the Hindu texts of Vedas—that is Vedanta, which means realising the divinity within, through the process of self-realisation. And his

Vedanta interpretation conflicted with ritualistic interpretation of the Vedas by what is known as the *Purva Mimamsa* School of thought. In Sankara's times, Mandana Mishra was the most popular exponent of the ritualistic *Purva Mimamsa* School of thought. Mandana Mishra was a householder and Sankara was a *Sanyasi* [Ascetic].

The dialogue between Sankara, the exponent of Vedanta, and Mandana Mishra, the exponent of ritualism, was very unique in more than one way. The stakes were too high for both—and would completely make their mission in life meaningless if the result is against them. If he was defeated in the dialogue, Mandana Mishra, a householder, would renounce family life and the world and become an ascetic. And if Sankara was defeated, he would have to renounce being an ascetic, to become a householder. Besides the high and unique stakes, the other unique feature of the dialogue was that the umpire who to decide who was the winner and who was the loser was Mandana Mishra's wife—Ubaya Bharati. How did she execute her responsibility was even more unique. She made both Sankara and Mandana Mishra wear fresh garland and said the one whose garland loses freshness would be the loser in the dialogue—the reason being that if garland loses its freshness, it means the person who adorns it had become angry because of the heat generated in his body by the dialogue would cause the flowers to lose their freshness. That means if you become angry, you have lost in the dialogue. In Ubaya Bharati's method of judging, no judge is needed and no one needs to be judged as wrong or as right. That is the high discipline of dialogue. That is why we named dialogue as SAMVAD, on the standards of Adishankara and Mandana Mishra. There is no need for anger, there's only need for logic, need for facts. There's nothing which can convince the world like facts because logic stands on facts.

Internalised Dialogue—Avoids Violence in Streets

The Hindu-Buddhist tradition of dialogue sans anger and hate has led to a society sans discord and violence. Hinduism constitutes a commonwealth of diverse—millions of diverse varieties of—faiths and practices. This commonwealth of religions is secured not by just tolerance but by mutual acceptance and recognition of diversities. This mutual acceptance is procured by dialogue among learned masters. If there is peace between religious masters, there would be peace between Gods. Peace between Gods will ensure peace between their adherents. Peace between Gods is the only thing that will guarantee peace between people. If Gods are seen fighting, the people who swear on them are bound to fight. That is precisely what Hindu-Buddhist traditions avoided by the *Tarka Shastra* model of dialogue. The dialogue model made Hindu-Buddhist thought systems recognise not only difference among believers, but also the existence of non-believers. Actually, classical Hinduism classified Buddhism which does not believe in Vedas, itself as non-believing faith, but recognised its right to be so. This is because Hinduism itself had experienced non-believing materialist thinkers like Chruvaka and Bahuka who advised living well on the earth is the only purpose of life.

The Adi Sankara-Mandana Mishra dialogue was also an illustration of how different philosophies can co-exist or converge through dialogue. It was a beautiful exposition of how different thoughts, sourced from different masters, can co-exist with differences. Also, there may be a communication gap between master and disciple. Every master may be right, but every disciple need not be. The original master may have communicated properly to his disciple, but the way successive disciples communicated it and recommunicated over 2000 years, may have deviated from what the original master had intended, in today's practice. Miscommunications are, and can be carried forward in this way. Dialogue on the *Tarka Shastra* model, contemporaneously modified and restated by Hans Kung has the potential to overcome all miscommunication arising by the exhaustion and fatigue of time. Dialogue also helps to expose the wrong fundamentals to be cosmetic so their centrifugal potential is preserved for posterity. It is this examination of the fundamentals through *Purva Paksha* dialogue which continues even today in Hindu traditions that has avoided clashes in the streets. The *purva paksha* tradition continues even today within Hinduism as self-criticism. For example in the temples of South India, discussions are carried out among the disciples of Rama, who worship him as an Avatar, on whether he was right in sending his wife Sita to forest and whether he was right in killing the monkey King Vali in the way he did. It means that even Rama considered as an Avatar of God was not beyond comment. This is what has made Hinduism a philosophic religion—almost saying that the other view may be equally right. This is one of the important reasons for the bewilderingly diverse India being the most dynamic democracy. Because Hinduism allowed for its fundamentals and even God to be examined, is why despite the vast and the bewildering complexity of India, it could absorb contemporary democracy well into its polity. If you put India on the one side and rest of the world on the other, you see more diversity in India. And yet

India has a record of being the only country which does not have a history of mass violence or anarchy or state violence against people.

The research done by Prof RJ Rummel on mass killings of humans all over the world for the last 2500 years shows that in India till the 13th century [when religious invaders struck at India] there was virtually little violence and killing. Against over 680 million at the minimum, and 1.2 billion maximum killings of humans estimated for the world by Rummel, in 2500 years the estimated killing in India was not even two hundred thousands! This harmony continues in contemporary India even today, thanks to the inherited quality of dialogue and discussions rather than street fight and violence. India has only 12,800 police stations for a total of 6,68,000 villages and towns and yet figures among the countries with the least amount of human violence and crime against humans. Because of its acceptance of all ways of worship and ways of life it has developed very high acceptance levels, not just tolerance. India has a tradition of boasting 33,00,00,000 Gods which at one point of time was more than the population of Hindus and so it could easily accept a few more Gods provided the existing Gods in India are not disturbed! India can invent new Gods and accept any God from outside.

Swami Vivekananda said that India never believed in the model to have a boxing match on whether your God is right or mine. Today bombs are thrown to kill and assert the superiority of Gods. It is therefore natural to Hindu-Buddhist traditions to listen to the most disagreeable view point without disrespecting its exponent. If someone said Adi Sankara is wrong, he will not be killed or even abused. Likewise if somebody says Buddha is wrong there will be no violence. This element is absent in most other religious traditions of the world. On the contrary there is fundamentalist pressure to assert only my faith as true and others' as false. This is where Hans Kung model becomes relevant for dialogue. It is the responsibility of the Hindu Buddhist traditions to take this initiative and make SAMVAD a platform where facts will be spoken very plainly and with responsibility and without anger and hate. That is why in SAMVAD II a roundtable of religious people has been conceived where they can discuss the fundamentals of religions in a calm and peaceful atmosphere without being misunderstood, for the common good, for the world and for each other. This is a conflict avoidance mechanism that goes to the root of the conflicts to root them out. The world needs it today more than at any other point of time in the past. Today all nations, all governments want peace. But the people—religious, faithful people—are at war. Conflict avoidance is more important than conflict resolution.

Dialogue to Harmony to Security

Dialogue—open, transparent, sans anger and hate—leads to harmony among faiths even with differences. It is harmony that best guarantees security. Security bereft of harmony is a short-term idea. Short term security is the State's gun vs the terrorists' gun issue in cases where the underlying battle is religion driven disharmony. In that case, the hand that raises the gun against any state should be mercilessly dealt with. It is the function of the state to quell all violence including ideologically justified violence and anarchy by counter violence. This cannot be dispensed with, particularly in modern times when cross border driven terrorism is rocking nation-states. But that can only be a short-term measure. The durable long-term measure is, as Hans Kung said, harmony through dialogue between faiths secured by open dialogue. This is the function of the spiritual masters and transpolitical social leaders. This is where Samvad steps in, to initiate the long haul process without which conflicts cannot be avoided. Avoidance of conflicts calls for dialogue, and dialogue has to be honest, open, truthful dialogue. Long term security is possible only by exclusive faiths realising that they cannot homogenise the diverse world by one faith. This is possible only by dialogue. This has to originate in Asia which is the home of Hinduism and Buddhism, the two philosophic religions.

Environmental Consciousness

And the next global issue is environment. Today we are at war with nature, nature is also reacting in a big way. Humans cannot be independent of nature. There is interdependence between humans and nature. Man is not to exploit and enjoy nature. Creation is not Anthropocentric. It is Ecocentric. Man is integral to nature. World today functions on anthropocentric model—with humans at the centre and nature as his supporting periphery. In the scheme of integrality of creation, human beings are not at the centre, but a part, of nature. This is the crux of Hindu and Buddhist philosophy which regard nature as sacred. One instance to show how nature is not just loved in India, but revered and even supreme sacrifices are made to protect nature, happened in the Indian state of Rajasthan, in 1782— which is part of the recent and recorded history. The Maharaja of Jodhpur sent an army in the forest to cut trees for refurnishing his new palace. Members of a local community—Bishnois—who have taken a lifetime vow to protect trees resisted it. A lady belonging to the Bishnoi community first started the resistance with two kids and protested against the trees being cut. The army said "we will cut you" if you stopped us. She said "you cut us" before you cut the trees and saying so she hugged the tree along with two kids. The arrogant and angry soldiers cut the lady and the two children and hundreds of others from the community rushed to the spot and hugged the trees and the army killed over 360 people and yet had to return without cutting any tree. The history goes on to say that the King profusely apologised for the barbarous act and compensated them heavily for the wrong done. Can one see a greater illustration of the spiritual and emotional connect between man and nature than the philosophy that makes people sacrifice their lives for nature? This emanates out of the philosophy expounded in the *Isavasya* Upanishad which says "*Isavasyam Idam Sarvam*" which was translated by Mahatma Gandhi as meaning 'everything down to the tiniest atom is manifestation of the divine'—not just man.

This is the deep ecological consciousness that the Hindu philosophy expounds. This cannot be brought about by any government, even with a 100% mandate. Government can regulate and coerce human obedience by law but cannot force people into environmental consciousness. Consciousness stems from within and it is a product which shapes the behaviour of those who adhere to it. The consciousness brings about emotional connect with nature. Some Scandinavian environmental thinkers call it deep environmental consciousness. And that is why we want spiritual masters from different religious streams to take up and lead this as a serious issue. I was talking to Swami Avdheshananda Maharaj who heads the *Hindu Dharma Acharya Sabha,* a platform of ancient Hindu institutions. I told him I am not the legitimate voice of Hindu philosophy. What he and Hindu exponents like him speak is only legitimate as millions of people listen to him and follow him. It is he and people like him who must expound the views I have expressed more authentically and with legitimacy.

My appeal is to all religious and spiritual heads to make conflict avoidance and environmental consciousness a mass movement through their reach.

(Mr S Gurumurthy is Chairman, Vivekananda International Foundation)

2

ANIRBAN GANGULY

I represent an organisation that is named after a politician, but a politician-statesman who was one of the most dynamic presidents of the Maha Bodhi Society of India—Dr. Syama Prasad Mookerjee.

Therefore, it is highly symbolic that I stand here today representing him, in a sense. I also wish to point out that Dr. Syama Prasad Mookerjee was the one, through whose intervention, the sacred relics of Mahamoggallana and Sariputta, the two chief disciples of Buddha were given as a permanent loan by the Government of India to the people of Myanmar. These were enshrined at the sacred Kaba Aye Pagoda in March 1951. Therefore for me, it is doubly symbolic when I come back to Myanmar, because I look back at this history and I am reminded of the letter that Prime Minister U Nu wrote to Dr. Mookerjee when Sariputta and Moggallana's relics were enshrined here. He said that the people and the Government of Myanmar, Burma at that time, would be infinitely grateful to you and he ended his letter with '*sadhu, sadhu, sadhu.*' That precious letter is still preserved in one of the leading public libraries in New Delhi.

In the context of the theme of *Samvad*, I stand here to share a few thoughts and perspectives. I have developed this theory of coalitions of civilisations and cultures and coalitions of civilisational states. It is through these coalitions of civilisations and cultures that we can evolve our unique model of conflict avoidance, inspired by the wisdom that is inherent in our spirituality and traditions.

Friends and elders, I want to tell you something very interesting. I think there has never been a better moment in India than today. India aspires, India does not worry. Under the dispensation led by Prime Minister Modi, in the last three years, it is a civilisational India that is waking up. There is aspiration, there is hope, and there is opportunity. Nowhere in the last six decades have we heard an Indian Prime Minister standing on the ramparts of the iconic Red Fort in Delhi and speaking about equality, social justice and about the need to empower all sections of society through affirmative and positive action in the customary Independence Day speech which is delivered on 15th August every year. This approach of compassion, of humanism, of *Karuna*, of empathy, of resolve to empower the marginalised through equity and justice is what reflects the reawakening, a reiteration, of the spirit and ideals of Buddha in the land of his birth. Therefore, if there is one country today about which we need not worry, it is India. That is because India aspires to integrate her civilisational knowledge, her spiritual strength, and to work from within to regenerate herself. She aspires to take her position of equality in the comity of nations.

I have this propensity of connecting. It is Swami Vivekananda who had breathed this sense of patriotism in India when we were a colonial state. Since then, we have come back to a cycle. Indian nationalism in its essence is not predatory. Unlike the West, Indian nationalism is assimilative. Mahatma Gandhi and Swami Vivekananda saw no conflict between nationalism and internationalism. What we see today in India and what Prime Minister Modi said this morning is a beautiful, harmonious amalgamation of India's message of nationalism wedded to her vision of internationalism. Dr. Ananda Coomaraswamy, one of the foremost scholars and philosophers that India has produced, Swami Vivekananda, Sri Aurobindo were just some of the Masters who symbolised and defined that balance and harmony of nationalism and internationalism. I argue that all Indic religions, all nations that have been inspired by Buddha and by the middle path of the Master, are uniquely situated to blend this nationalism and internationalism. Therefore, friends, let us not be worried but let us aspire.

While standing here, I am reminded of Swami Ranganathananda, the President of the Ramakrishna Mission, who between 1939 and 1942 served as the Secretary of the Mission here, in Rangoon. What did Swami Ranganathananda say about the Master? He said, "When the great message of Buddha throbbed in the hearts of millions of our country, the whole nation arose morally as also politically. With that accession of strength, our nation became the centre for a wide and rich cultural diffusion in the world outside."

I think that is exactly what is happening in India now, there is an accession of strength, a realisation that our rich cultural tradition and spiritual wisdom can sustain our collective and multi-dimensional rise as a civilisational state.

While inaugurating the first *Samvad*, where the Most Venerable Sitagu Sayadaw was also present with him on the dais, Prime Minister Modi observed "They say this century is going to be the Asian century. I am very clear that without embracing the path and ideals shown by Buddha, this century cannot be an Asian century." In turning this into an Asian century, I think the civilisational coalition and the cultural coalition inspired by the messages of the Eastern Masters are imperative. Dr. Syama Prasad Mookerjee himself had said that, "Gautama Buddha gave the world his message of love, peace and understanding 2,500 years ago in a simple manner, which carried faith and conviction not only to the learned, but what is more which carried hope and aspiration to the masses of people." It is that hope and aspiration which in a conflict-ridden world, is again being rekindled. India and Myanmar today are ideal representatives of that aspiration of the millions.

It is very fascinating when one reads that Swami Vivekananda had a very special relationship with Buddha. His '*Buddha Bhakti*', as I have termed it, was so intense and alive that he focused on studying the development of Buddhism through its various stages. Many of his lectures were devoted to the subject of examining Buddhism and Hinduism, their inter-related and complex history. Vivekananda talked about Buddha very often. When he talked about Buddha, he did it with the deepest feeling so that those who heard him felt the very presence of Buddha. In his characteristic style he once said, "I am the servant of the servants of the servants of Buddha. Who was ever like him, the Lord, who never performed one action for himself?"

You obviously know that when Swami Vivekananda took *sanyasa*, the first place he visited was Bodh Gaya. The last place, in the last winter of his life that he visited was Bodh Gaya. At the World Parliament of Religions, it was Anagarika Dharmapala and Swami Vivekananda who formed a formidable alliance in defence of Indic faiths. Each defended the other when they were attacked either by their countrymen or those present. It is very interesting, I just want to narrate this anecdote here, though anecdotal narration is not part of research. I would still like to say it here. It is said that Anagarika Dharmapala asked a large audience outside the Hall of Columbus, where the Parliament had convened, as to how many of them had read the life of Buddha. Only five people responded affirmatively in that large audience. Dharmapala in his inimitable style shouted, "Five only! Four hundred and seventy five millions of our people accept our religion of love and hope, and you call yourselves a great nation? And yet you do not know the history of this great teacher? How dare you judge us?" This was Dharmapala, and some of you may know that he went out of his way to defend Swami Vivekananda.

Now, I'm making these points simply because I'm trying to link thoughts. I say that Buddhism and Hinduism as interpreted and represented by Swami Vivekananda have both a special role, mission and task ahead under this rubric of conflict avoidance. Prime Minister Modi has often said, in fact he has used the phrase "challenges to sustainable world peace." I think in India today there is a lot of fundamental thinking going on. It is very interesting to recall in this context of the theme of conflict avoidance that, on his first visit to the US in September 2014, in an interaction with scholars at the Council of Foreign Relations in New York, Prime Minister Modi made a very important observation. For those who actually understand the potent of that observation, there is a deeper line there. He said that it is ideologies that are in conflict with each other, but philosophies transcend ideologies. The inherent nature of philosophies is to try and discover the meeting grounds.

We in India today are very concretely and pragmatically trying to discover the way that inspires and guides us to philosophical action and not ideological conflict. It is because we are trying to discover that action, that inherent resistances rise from various quarters. Ultimately, it is philosophies that triumph and not ideologies. However this is a very interesting and bold statement that he made in his first major exposure to a foreign audience as Prime Minister. So my submission is that the menace of terrorism in our region and beyond is a stark manifestation of, as Prime Minister Modi says, mindsets. The problems are not because there are conflicts between nation-states, the problem is that of a mindset. It is that mindset that we first need to address in order to be able to avoid conflict.

My submission is that we need to form civilisational coalitions and cultural coalitions. In trying to do this, we will perceive that there are countries uniquely situated to coalesce and collaborate with each other. In the context of India and Myanmar, there are a number of strands that bind us civilisationally and in more modern terms—with the advent of Swami Vivekananda and with the restatement of our civilisational vision as inspired by Buddha. We need to discover that. *Samvad*, as Professor Gurumurthy observed this morning, has to expand and extend itself into a multi-dimensional structure. It has to be an ongoing process. As long as the process of *Samvad* is a continuing one, friends, we need not be worried. We need to aspire and definitely reassert that finally, in the evolution of mankind it is the philosophies, world views and belief systems which talk about a higher destiny for humanity, which look at the underlying fundamental unity of global living, which speak of synergy and harmony, are not exclusivist and ideology driven are the ones which will sustain themselves in the long run. It is these that are going to survive and finally be victorious.

(Dr Anirban Ganguly is Director, Dr Syama Prasad Mookerjee Research Foundation, New Delhi)

3

H.R.S.D. Mitrapala

IT is a great pleasure and privilege for me to stand here and speak a few words representing Sri Lanka. I bring with me 21 million greetings from the people of Sri Lanka, who take keen interest in dialogue, and in engaging deeply with people of all faiths, towards building bridges and creating peace and harmony amongst diversity of peoples and nations in the world.

As you know, Sri Lanka and Myanmar have had a long-standing historic relationship that goes back several centuries. As two pioneer Theravada Buddhist countries in the world, both Sri Lanka and Myanmar have been bound together in an inseparable bond of friendship and brotherhood. Whenever there has been any threat to *Buddhashasana* or the monastic order, both our countries have looked to each other for the sustenance and furtherance of the Buddha *dhamma,* and for the well being of all. I therefore, am proud and thrilled to be here and speak a few words in this conference today.

We are living in the second decade of twenty-first century, in which the world has seen an unprecedented level of scientific and technological advancement. Mobile revolution and social media have completely eclipsed the human race and consciousness. Such modernity however, does not necessarily bring much needed peace, harmony, well-being, or happiness. On the contrary, what we are witnessing today is a rapid decline of moral and ethical values as well as a lack of respect and understanding amongst continents, countries, nations, religions and so forth.

Buddhism and Hinduism, as the two oldest faith traditions in the world, have had a major impact in bringing about peace and harmony to the hearts and minds of millions of people over the world through mindfulness, meditation, Yoga and contemplation at the individual level, while also creating world peace amongst countries and nations. Our two faith traditions have so much to offer to the world in the spirit of *ahimsa* or non-violence, and *karuna* or the spirit of compassion, which truly are the founding stones of our two faiths.

With regard to conflict avoidance and conflict resolutions, the Buddha *dhamma* in particular has so much to offer to the world today. As the Enlightened One, the Buddha has admonished, on many occasions, all conflicts arising from human minds and thoughts, before they can get translated into conflicts across nations and countries, world wars and global disputes. It is therefore absolutely essential, as the Buddha himself pointed out, that we trace all conflicts to their roots, which indeed ultimately boil down to three poisons in the human heart—greed, hatred and delusion.

If there is to be any peace in the world, it is paramount that peace and harmony is first established in the very roots they arise from, that is, in the hearts and minds of human beings. Once the Buddha pointed out that those who are attached to fixed views and opinions are bound to carry on with nothing but conflicts and disharmony towards each other. '*Sakkuncha dittanche aggahe sangha, thegate anta chiraante loke.*' It is therefore quite timely that we the followers of those noble words of wisdom and compassion, gather together and deliberate in such conferences and meetings to decide how best we could contribute to world peace in the interest of all concerned.

As you know, the entire world is interested in learning about Yoga, meditation and towards developing more tolerance, respect and understanding each other. In this regard, mindfulness and Yoga have become key and there is growing interest and much enthusiasm in Buddhist and Hindu practices across the world today. I would like to conclude by recalling another noble saying of the great teacher, '*sammadida gudajanan averenecha sammanti isadhammo sanantano*', which means that 'hatred can never cease through hatred but by love alone which is the perennial truth'. We would like to wish you all our very best on behalf of the people and Government of Sri Lanka. May the world be a better place for all of us to live in.

(H.R.S.D. Mitrapala is the Deputy Minister of Buddha Sasana & Justice, Govt of Sri Lanka)

4

Surin Pitsuwan

IT is a great privilege and a personal honour for me to be standing in front of you people from various faiths from Asia and other corners of the world. The introduction that Madame had just made about me missed one thing, and that is I am a Muslim in a majority Buddhist kingdom. The fact that I became the Foreign Minister of Thailand for three plus years between 1997 and 2001 reflects something about the people of Thailand. That is that mutual trust and confidence in each other are very important for societal and national harmony.

I have been working as a politician. This afternoon Professor Gurumurthy didn't really give much credit to politicians, but not all politicians are bad. In fact, if you want to solve all problems of the world, you need them too. Partly, because they too have their own followers. So, if you have the right kind of consciousness that Professor Gurumurthy was talking about, the right kind of awareness, passion and compassion, you can also depend on conscientious politicians. I think you would count Nehru as a politician. I think in some way, in many ways, you would count Mahatma Gandhi as a politician. They were just of different kinds, different moulds and different modes of leadership. Not only were they conscientious about their human responsibility towards their own people, but also towards the entire world and humanity.

Now, this very conference is a reflection of the fact that we do need each other. That we are not only bent on a collision course, or confrontation or a clash of civilisations. The fact that the theme and inspiration of this Samvad I and II, and I had the privilege of attending one in Tokyo in the middle of last year. The inspiration for Samvad came from a Catholic theologian, Hans Kuntz, who said there shall be no peace until there is peace among religions. There can be no peace among religions until there are dialogues. There can be no meaningful substantive dialogue until you have the understanding of the fundamentals and the substance of all those religions that you want to enter into a dialogue with. So the very inspiration of this Samvad is already inter-faith and is already drawing the best from the leaders of a different faith. From mind, from yours and many others.

Let us settle one point, and that point is not civilisational clash that we are travelling toward, but it should be a civilisational accommodation—A mutual respect and mutual confidence. Now, I don't know if you are familiar with one methodology of studying comparative religions. I think this methodology can help us in our journey towards harmony together. In this little planet, there are now 7.3 billion of us. In 32 years or in 2050 there will be 2 billion more, 9.3 billion. Yes, Professor Gurumurthy, if we don't evolve that new consciousness, if we don't develop that new awareness and I would call it global awareness and global consciousness. The consciousness that we belong to this little planet together. The consciousness that we own this little planet together, not just the rich, poor or middle but every one of us. All 7.3 billion, each and every one of us owns this little planet and we need to take care of it.

But then there is diversity among us, and how we manage that diversity such that it would be a source of creativity and a source of mutual confidence and a source of understanding and harmony among us, will be critical. There is that approach to comparative religion that I would like to raise with you and leave with you so that you can think about this leaving this conference and Samvad. That approach is called 'transcendental unity of religions.' Meaning at one level, there is one fundamental truth, but articulated, taught or described by different prophets, leaders, gurus or intellectuals in the contexts appropriate to their own people, history and environment.

I come from Southern Thailand, where there was a very, very, respectable monk among all Thai and foreigners who believe in Buddhism. His name was Buddhasa Bhikku, or slave of Lord Buddha. He coined this phrase. He said there are two languages that have somehow led us into conflict and misunderstanding and caused mutual hatred among us. One is the language of *dhamma*. When the Muslims speak the language of *dhamma* it is the same *dhamma*. When the Hindus speak the language of *dhamma*, it is the same truth. When the Buddhists speak of *dhamma*, it is the same truth. It is the same lofty truth for all humanity. But we got caught in this symbolism of trying to articulate that highest truth. Buddhasa Bhikku called it human language, and those of you who speak Thai or understand it, '*pha sat dhamma, pha sat khon*'. The language of *dhamma* and the language of human beings.

When we speak the language of human beings, we argue about what hell looks like, we argue about what heaven looks like, we argue about sin and we argue about virtue. But when we speak the language of *dhamma*, goodness, practising *dhamma*, detachment, no self, compassion, *mahta*, *karuna*, *mudita*, *ubekha*, all these features of *dhamma* are the same. Let us resolve at Samvad II here, that we should not get caught in the differences of language and symbolism with which we try to articulate our truth.

A Zen master once compared this dilemma of the language of human beings and the language of *dhamma* in this way, which some of you might have heard before. He said, 'If you use your index finger to point at the moon in the early evening, a dog would look at your index finger. Because a dog doesn't understand the abstraction and the object that this index finger points to.' He said, 'But a human being with intelligence will not look at the index finger, but look at the moon, because that's where this index finger is pointing.' Therefore let us not be caught in the diversity of the symbolism of the languages that we use to describe that moon. Let us look at the moon, let us understand the moon and that's when I think we can find the transcendental unity of religions.

And yes, this morning there was one point which I think was extremely important and I will stop after that. That point is, let us have a sense of humility in each and every one of us. That after all, we are fallible human beings. We are not owners of the truth alone, absolute and nobody else. We may be 75 per cent right and 25 per cent wrong or 50 per cent wrong and 50 per cent right. Let us allow others to also have the right to be wrong and be right and that would lead to a sense of humility. That I am humble enough to know that I don't own the truth alone. There are others who see it differently, maybe the same thing but describes it differently because of the human language and *dhamma* language. Let me tell you that this is not an Asiatic wisdom. It may be ours too, but it is not absolutely ours alone.

Socrates said the same thing, that 'I know nothing. I am only a seeker of the truth. I am not in possession of the truth.' But I respect your way and you should respect my way, therefore the dialogues of Plato describing how Socrates walked in the *agora* (the marketplace) of Athens, seeking people who know more than he did. At the end he said he found none. Well, we can assume that yes, he was probably the most intelligent human being at that time, but he did not foreclose the possibility that others probably could also share a glimpse of the truth just like he did. That is philosophical humility. I think if all religious leaders and followers can live with our neighbours with that sense of humility, that you too have the right to be right and to be wrong, just like me and every one of us. I think harmony is within reach and dialogue with humility will lead us there.

(Late Dr Surin Pitsuwan was former DG, ASEAN and Former Foreign Minister of Thailand)

5

Balbir Punj

BEFORE me at least two speakers have referred to Mr. Hans and I cannot begin my presentation without referring to him. What did this Roman Catholic church official say? Which Mr. Gurumurthy referred to, as did another speaker. He said that, "Peace among nations is not possible without peace among religions. Peace among religions is not possible without dialogue among religions. Dialogue among religions is impossible without investigating the fundamentals of different religions." This is what the concept paper of Samvad says, this is also what the speaker had said and this is precisely what has not been done since morning. We have not looked into the fundamentals of religions which have been causing problems, not only in this century but in centuries before as well.

Ladies and gentlemen, I come from India. We have been at war almost for the last 70 years. The British left in 1947 and before they left, they divided the country. When they did so, the division was bloody, leaving a minimum of a million (10 lakh) people killed and at least 10 million homeless and displaced, who had to be transported from one side of the border to the other and vice versa. It is from there that our struggle starts and it continues even today. We have been in a latent war, ever since. Our northern-most province is called Kashmir. Kashmir is a region where there is a shootout almost every day. There has been ethnic cleansing of a community called Kashmiri Pandits to the last man, in the last 20 years. It is very painful that this has been happening in a country which for the last few thousand years has always preached peace and evolved systems and paradigms where you can put up happily with differences.

When somebody says that Indians are tolerant, I protest. We are not tolerant people. We are people who accept differences or ignore differences. When you say that you are a tolerant country, or I am tolerant, it implies that somewhere I don't like the way you look or the way you pray or speak or eat, or even a combination of all this. We accept people as they are. It happens among us in our society every day. In a family of five, three persons may be worshipping three different deities. One may go to Hanuman ji's temple, another may go to a Ram temple and a third to a Devi temple. The remaining two may not have faith in god(s) or may not be believers. Despite this, you will not find any complication or problem amongst them. They would be living as peacefully as if all five believe in one God. After having been brought up in such a culture and then having to deal with a situation where people are killed because of their faith, it becomes very contradictory.

If we go back in history, Buddha was born in India. Not born in India technically, in Lumbini in present-day Nepal. However, his enlightenment came in India. It is where he practiced Buddhism and gave his message and that was about 2,500 years ago. Christ was born 500 years later in another part of the world. Now ladies and gentlemen, you please compare the way Buddha was treated by his contemporary society, despite the fact that he preached something very different from what was the norm at the time and the way Christ was treated by his contemporary society for having preached something which was unacceptable to the people there. We have lived with this tradition ever since. The essence of our philosophy is that we don't see any difference between us and our gods. We treat our gods as our mirror image, therefore we are not scared of our gods. We are not scared of them. We love them, worship them and we also go to them when we have problems. Occasionally we try to strike deals with them as well, that if you do me this favour I will do this for you. Let me tell you, we are not scared of our gods.

As Gurumurthy ji very rightly pointed out there could be as many gods as number of Hindus. Everybody can have a god or goddess of their own choice. We also believe in the theory of *karma*. If we love god or worship gods, it is not with a view that we can get back favours. Karmic theory states that 'as you sow, so shall you reap'. We will get rewarded or punished as per our *karma*. This extends further, in that we see an extension of god(s) in everything around us, as has been pointed out by some earlier speakers. We see god in leaves, forests, stones, and animals. We think and believe that we are part of god and these things, whether they be stones or animals are part of us. The entire universe is integrated. The entire universe is one. This is where our love or concern for the environment stems from. This comes from our traditions and extends from *dharti mata* or the earth as mother and all the way to the sun, moon and galaxy.

Despite this sort of philosophy, unfortunately our experience with the rest of the world has not been very kind. We could never imagine that somebody, a chap called Bakhtiyar Khilji in 1193 and march straight to Nalanda. It was an 800-year-old university at that time, with 20,000 residential scholars and almost 2,000 teachers. That this guy will come with a horde of armed horsemen, attack the university, kill the scholars, force them to flee and then ask a question—'why this big library consisting of thousands of books?' was unthinkable. The answer given to him was this was *ilm* or knowledge (this is knowledge). To which he responded that all knowledge was contained in his religious book. The book given to him by his prophet contained the knowledge of the entire world. Now the intelligent question was if all the books had the same knowledge which his religious book had, then what was the justification of having that many books when knowledge could be gleaned from just his one book. If the knowledge contained in those books was different or they preached something different from what was in his religious book, then it was blasphemy. In either case Khilji concluded the books had no business to be there. He was parked there for eight months along with his army. They never went to collect fuel to cook their food, they used the books to feed the fires that ran their kitchens. From there Khilji continued on to Udaigiri, Dharamshila and with that the institutionalised system of learning came to an end.

This process continues, as I was mentioning, through Kashmir. There has been a lot of terrorist action and incidents in Mumbai, Delhi, Bangalore and more cities. You mention a place and it is there. Now, it is happening in European cities like London, Paris etc you name it. No part of the world seems to be secure. Those who are indulging in these terrorist activities claim that their inspiration comes to them from their scripture. I am not saying it, I am no scholar of Islam. They claim this and have been claiming this from Mohammad Bin Kasim's time, who attacked India in 712, right up to Osama Bin Laden and to the odd guy who drives around in Paris or London and kills innocent people. They all claim that their inspiration comes from their religious book and their religion. As the preamble of this conference says, quoting Hans that we must debate the fundamentals. After all, what is it that motivated Muhammad bin Qasim in 712 to attack India, and Mahmud Ghazni subsequently to invade India over 13 to 15 times within 32 years of his rule.

From then to Osama bin Laden and from him to a whole lot of people now who go and kill themselves so that they can kill others. Their hatred for non-believers is to the extent that they are willing to die a violent death just to bring death to them.

Is it not our duty, the duty of all those who strive for world peace and harmony to look into the basics of the religion and come to some conclusion and say, this is acceptable and this is not acceptable? Gurumurthy ji gave a very good example. Hinduism has the slur of untouchability. Right from Guru Nanak to Gandhi ji, to Veer Savarkar to Dr. Hedgewar—each one of them has said, even Vivekananda, even if it has been said by God that untouchability is justified, we don't accept it. The state of India has taken every possible step to eradicate its evils. We had the problem of Sati, occasionally women would get so charged by tradition that when their husband died they would walk up to his pyre and burn themselves on it. This was completely inhuman, and our society revolted. There have been mythological instances, some justification in some scriptures. But Hindu society took a united stand irrespective of what is contained in scriptures, we would not accept it. You go through the Bible there could be many problem areas. Western society doesn't accept many of the things mentioned in it. They may not have publicly disowned them, but they have distanced themselves from many of the practices in it. If Hinduism can do it, if Christianity can do it, why is it that we cannot go into the fundamentals of Islam, debate with them and engage them in dialogue? If they are found to be inconsistent with the modern value systems, why can't appeal to them to drop them?

(Mr. Balbir Punj is a former two-term Member of the Upper House of the Indian Parliament)

6

Khin Maung Nyunt

THE theme "Peace, Harmony and Security" is not the theme of our time. It has always been the theme throughout history of mankind. Mankind has always been vexed with the problems of Peace, the problem of Harmony and problem of security. Histories of civilizations are nothing but the stories of keeping peace, maintaining harmony and security, successes and failures and continued human efforts at them.

To-day in our present Age of Globalization of our 21st Century we are continuing our efforts at solving these problems as our forefather had done in the past.

To-day here at this gathering we have representatives of faiths or religions who each by themselves have their way of trying to meet these problems. Through peace, harmony and security. We are sure to find common means of achieving our common goals, regardless of seemingly divergences and differences. At the end of our three days of dialogue, I am confident that we would get common ideas or means to get to our common goals.

Please allow me to present how Theravada Buddhism, which I profess, tries to get peace, harmony and security. Lord Gautama Buddha in his lifetime had made many successful efforts to settle the international, inter-ethnic, inter-clan and inter-faiths conflicts in a peaceful way by means of avoiding extremes and keeping the middle way *Mezima Padipada* via. Media, the best way to solve any problem or conflict of any time anywhere. Extremes provoke resistance. The means should always be sought for permanent settlement and peace.

In line with Buddha's middle way, we of our century today, individually bilaterally, sub-regionally, regionally, internationally are trying our best to apply this middle way in our attempts to avoid armed conflict, to achieve harmony, peace and security. Negotiation, compromise, conciliations, the rule of international law, etc we are using at different levels of cooperation, such as G.M.S., BIMSTEC, ASEAN and its charter, UNO and its charter and several other associated international organizations and groups—G7, G20 etc are nothing but *mezima paddipada.*

To give just a few of Buddha's successes in the use of middle way in *rekita* harmony, peace and security, the following are cited. Although Buddhism in essence is final peace in life hereafter—*Wivaina*—the end of all suffering cravings and defilements—End of body and soul.

But Buddha's biography has many events and *suttans* (discourses) of his successes in settling disputes and problems and conflicts by means of middle way. *Maha Samayu Sutta* is one shining example of solving water dispute between two kingdoms of the Sabyu race on the River Yawhome in India. The *Sutta* emphasized the benefit of harmony and unity. The two kingdoms were salvaged from mutual destruction.

Same as the case with regard to *Metta Sutta* [Discourse on loving kindness to all sentient beings] which the Buddha delivered to his disciple monks on the Full moon of Wakhaung. His wa vows for rain retreat of monks was his way of respect for and preservation of mutual environment for all living creatures.

Mangala Sutta he gave at the behest of a deva at Jeturanna, the kingdom of Savathir, was his advice on human- and natural environment relations, between humans—Parents and Children, Teachers and Pupils, King and People. Monks and disciples etc are adviced to control *Loba* [greed], *dosa* [Anger] and *Moha* [ignorance] and practice calmness of mind when faced with the ups and downs of life. Simple and easy advices but must practice.

Buddha's teachings are not dogmactic. They are open to discussions, one must practice it only when one understands it. They are tolerant of other faiths as other faiths have the common end—Peace, harmony and security. So, in this way, Buddhism co-exists with other faiths.

Many of the UN Days—Peace Day, Environment Day, Democracy Day, Teacher's Day, Old Age Day, Mother's Day, Father's Day, Water Day etc. that we annually celebrate and observe are long preceded by the events and discourses of Buddha's time, e.g. the *Abhidhamma* Day or Fullmoon of *Thadingyut* is Buddha's Mother Day. After his discourse on *Abhidamma* to his mother who became a deva in the Taratimisa, he said he was returning his filial gratitude to his mother for his birth and milk she fed him. Buddha's revisit to his father King Sudhodanna of Kapilavastu on fullmoon Day of Tabaung was Buddha's Father Day. *Dhammucahys Sutta* Day delivered on the full moon of July was the fulfillment of his promise to his five forest recluses to share the truth of *dhamma* when he attains it. His conquest of 8 of his opponents by means of middle way of *metta* [loving kindness]—(1) The Meya, Satan, (2) Alava-Ku, the oyre (3) Zaevizamanz, the wicked women, (4) Nālāgiri the elephant sent by Peratalta, (5) Aungulimala, the notorious fore-finger cutter, (6) Thitsakaparapile who did not believe in *dhamma* (7) Nandawpananda the dragon who was a power monger and (8) Baka Brahma who thought he was permanently mortal. Buddha won their hearts by *metta sutta*, the middle way. *Metta Sutta* is the middle way. *Metta Sutta* calls for living together in peace of all sentient Peaceful Co-existence between nations regardless of differences in race, religion, or economic and socio-cultural systems. They (1) Respect each other's sovereignty (2) Territorial integrity; and practice (3) Non-aggression (4) Non-interference in internal affairs and (5) Peaceful coexistence. The mantra is to live and let live.

Mazima padipada the middle way is urgently needed in our time of globalization with many global problems and conflicts. All faiths have a common goal of peace, harmony and security. Let us work together by turning our back on biases, prejudices, and extreme views.

(Dr Khin Muang Nyunt is Professor Emeritus of International Relations, Yangon University)

7

Puneet Dalmia

I am neither a spiritual leader, nor a government representative, nor an academician but an ordinary citizen. I will approach this topic from the lens of a householder, what they call a *grihasta*. I am 44 years old and have two children who are going to be 13 and 10 years old this year. I was very interested in giving both of them good values, good *sanskaras* so that they can be good human beings. I was trying to talk to other parents from around the world to learn from them. One of my friends in USA told me that the big problems in schools 50 years ago were chewing gum, talking loudly in class, sometimes bunking classes and now the big problems in schools are teenage pregnancies, drug abuse and (believe it or not) shootouts. People kill each other with guns in schools.

Even in India, people are getting worried about what influence external forces will have on their kids. There is a lot of conflict people are dealing with even in raising children. If I look at families—there is double the income because two members are working, but half the time there is ten percent of the peace. There is materialistic prosperity but an emotional vacuum. If I look at society there is increased terrorism, increased conflict and people are not even sure whether they can go out in large cities after sunset without feeling a sense of danger. At all levels, whether it is individuals, families or as societies, we are dealing with enormous conflict. We are living in an era of unprecedented, exceptional progress but unprecedented conflict as well. I was thinking, why is this happening? What can we do about it?

I started thinking of who could provide the solution. Is it the most powerful people in the world, Presidents, Prime Ministers and heads of state? Many people in India, like me, start looking at the Western world for answers. Political leaders understand the pulse of society. Their election manifestos capture the moods and trends of society. I read a few election manifestos and many from the Western world promise a revival of family values. They promise to deliver, but are unable to do so. I was thinking family values are naturally present and nurtured in all Eastern civilisations. I grew up in a joint family. We were 30 of us living in one house. We shared rooms, toys, food and we even shared our clothes. I spent my childhood in an environment where we learned to accept and respect each other. We lived in harmony, there were differences but we accepted those. There were fights but we solved them very easily. We lived in harmony with a sense of ingrained love and compassion.

In a joint family, we also see the whole circle of life in the house without going outside the house. We see a young child, a young adult and old age. Subconsciously, it prepares you for life and makes you humble. It reduces ego and enhances acceptance. This is the experience that most family-oriented cultures naturally give to their children. In our society, as it was spoken earlier by many spiritual masters and leaders, the concept of family extends to community and society around us as seen in the *vasudhaiva kutumbakam* concept. My mother goes to Vrindavan, which is a religious city near New Delhi where I live. Once I went with her. It was noon and very hot outside. There was a beggar whose clothes were torn, his hair was unkept and he didn't get two square meals a day. I saw he was going to eat a *roti*. Suddenly a dog came and started salivating and looking at him. He tore the *roti* into half and fed one half to the dog. This is the normal soul and values which promote living in harmony with all beings. The concept of family extends to other creatures as well.

I live in a colony where there is one guy who runs a small shop. Every day he puts grains, water and biscuits for squirrels, dogs and birds. My father asked him once, "I feel you are very kind." He told him, "Sir, I am not kind, I am just giving these beings a share of my income which is something they deserve because they are a part of society. My grandparents have taught me that everybody has a share in my income and I am giving them their share. So, I'm not doing them a favour." The concept of family is extended to a larger society and all living beings. If this is the inner feeling towards all living beings, where is the scope for conflict with fellow humans? Our ancestors understood that family is the basic unit of society and civilisation. This is true in all Eastern civilisations. I'm a practitioner of Hinduism and in one line, if I can capture Hinduism—it is that everything, to the last atom is a manifestation of the divine. *Ishavasyam idam sarvam*. We see everything as an extension of God.

God is pervasive everywhere. This extends to nature as well. We worship trees, rivers, and mountains. Mr. Gurumurthy spoke about the Bishnoi movement in Rajasthan, where people killed themselves to save trees. Our Prime Minister, Mr. Modi and Prime Minister Abe have done the Ganga Aarti, where they worship the river and it's a very celebrated, energising ritual in Varanasi every day and in many other places in India. We visit Mount Kailash, which is supposed to be the ultimate pilgrimage in Hinduism. Respect for nature is part of our ancient beliefs. One of my friends told me that whatever we respect, we will use but not abuse. If you look at all ancient civilisations including Egypt which was one of the most prosperous civilisations, there was an inherent respect for nature. Many problems of climate change today are due to lack of reverence for Mother Nature. Accepting and respecting others and sensitivity towards all is natural to Eastern civilisations. Due to strong family roots and ancient beliefs that encourage harmony with nature, I think Eastern civilisations must come together and lead the dialogue for conflict avoidance and environmental consciousness.

It is a part of our shared Asian values with deep roots in our ancient sacred cultures. Leadership, I think, has to come from spiritual masters and religious leaders, not political leaders. I think political leaders think about the next election, while religious leaders think about the next generation. By and large, religious leaders have more credibility in today's world than political leaders. Religion has the enormous power to influence and unite millions of people. One of our greatest economists and political thinkers, Chanakya said that if any kingdom or civilisation has to survive and thrive, it has to stand on three pillars. The pillars of *satya* or truth, *nyaya* or justice and *dharma* or righteousness. I think Samvad II provides a platform for leaders of all faiths, and people who have no personal agenda to come together and deepen this dialogue for world peace and resurgence and establishment of *dharma* for the good of society.

I am very honoured to have been able to speak at Samvad and I really hope that many youngsters will get a chance to participate in this and hope that we can carry this dialogue forward to create a new consciousness around the world which will promote peace and establish *dharma*. Thank you.

(Mr. Puneet Dalmia is a philanthropist from India and Managing Director of Dalmia Bharat Group)

8

U Hla Maung

I feel much honour to speak a few words on this important occasion. May the blessing of the Almighty Lord be upon all of you.

The teachings of all major religions highlight the importance of inter-faith harmony for ensuring peace and co-existence of the people living in the world. If all the citizens of all nations are united without any discrimination of colour, creed, caste and if people of all religious communities respect each other, live amicably and work together we are sure to attain and accomplish economic progress at tremendous speed.

My first point is that when there is a focus on good-hearted religion in the country, then there is an advancement in the people, their understanding, their edicts, and their perspectives improve for the better. Every religion encourages peaceful co-existence against conflict. Islam also asks its followers to reach the goal of inter-faith harmony.

I will quote a few examples. Islam teaches us to accept all great spiritual leaders, enlightened ones, and messengers sent to this world in every age and time (Quran 16:36). Distinctions should not be made between these spiritual leaders (Quran 3:84). One should respect all religions and if necessary, one must defend and protect the peace and worship of different faiths (Quran 22:40). Do not abuse or revile those who believe in other than Allah (Quran 6:109). Make not mischief and disruption on the Earth (Quran 2:11). For every race Allah has made culture, tradition and civilisations which are beautiful and adorable (Quran 6:119). All mankind has been created from a single pair of male and female, then made into nations and tribes that you may know each other (Quran 49:14). All mankind you are but one family, your heart is one and no Arab is better than a non-Arab, nor is a white man better than a black man. The one who is righteous and truthful will be the most honoured among them. Therefore, the teachings of Holy Quran and Holy Prophet imply that Muslims have the duty to build inter-faith harmony.

Today all religions in the world are taking measures to build inter-faith harmony because they all have similar guidelines. My second point is the historic event of one Summit organised by the UN at its headquarters at the end of the twentieth century, where leaders of different religions and religious sects joined together to bring peace. I will take the liberty to quote from the speeches delivered then. Regarding avoiding conflict, it is badly needed for people to pursue this through inter-faith harmony and forbearance, instead of attempting to force their followers to convert to a particular faith. We, the people, should focus on the points of common interest which will be beneficial to all of mankind instead of activities that can provide disagreement and conflict based on the difference between religions. The essence of all religions is that everyone should be good-hearted. Religious and racial conflicts are largely due to misinterpretation and misunderstanding of religious teachings. At the Warsaw Millennium Summit, the program adopted was that the people of different faiths would pursue peace through inter-faith harmony.

My third point is that, religions have gradually emerged to bring advancements in human culture, habits, dignity and prosperity. Through scientific study of religions, religious scholars say that religion developed from fears and people started worshipping natural forces like the forests, mountains, land, air, sun, moon and oceans. Historically speaking such devotional ideologies started in Egypt, Babylon, Greece and Sumer. Theory and philosophy say that even during those days of the early religious systems, people had been less fearful and were less awed than the early man that inhabited the Earth before any kind of worship existed. After around 3000-2000 BC, the former religions were established. When religion became firmly established it brought culture and civilisation to mankind. The bestial nature of man reduced over the ages and centuries. Religious teachers and preachers explained and reminded us that if by luck religion had not come to us we would still be in the Dark Ages fighting and killing one another like animals.

As explained above, we can easily understand as to how much we have gradually improved and now, in the age of the twenty-first century, when we first start to think of each other as brothers of the same law, living in harmony and mutual respect in this global village without any distinction of colour or religion, we now have as little conflict as possible. Hence with the perfect understanding that every religion propagates correct principles, let us resolve to join together and bring peace, prosperity through a unity of all religious leaders and stand together as an example for future generations.

(Mr U Hla Maung is Senior Advisor, Myanmar Institute of Strategic & International Studies, Yangon)

9

Al-Haj U Aye Lwin

IT is indeed not at all surprising that the institutes representing the two peaceful religions, namely The Vivekananda International Foundation (VIF, New Delhi) and Sitagu International Buddhist Academy (SIBA, Yangon) have jointly initiated the Conference on Dialogue for Peace, Harmony and Security. Infact the theme of the conference is extremely relevant in present time where Peace and Harmony are the only remedy for the survival of our Planet at Earth.

I would like to fully endorse the concept that Hindu and Buddhist Philosophies accept other thoughts believe system as valid for their respective followers which make them doctrinally tolerant. It is also heartening to know that the organizers are of the opinion that all religions promote peace. This undeniable fact is testified by none other than one of the greatest soul to ever appear on earth, Sri Sri Rama Krishna Paramahansa (1836-1886).

Swami Saradana, a direct disciple of Ramakrishna, compiled an epic account of his master's life and Swami Chetananda has given as superb new translation of that, called Ramakrishna and Divine Play. Chatanada tells us that according to Ramakrishna, all religions are equally valid. He found a place for each one in his own life. He first realized God by following Hindu Practices, and then by following the Muslim and Christian path. Swami ji emphatically stressed that Sri Sri Ramakrishna Parahansa never spoke a harsh word against anyone's faith. He was so all embracing that member of every sect thought that he was one of them. He practiced a wide variety of religious expression and advocated for positive acceptance of other faiths, and also resolved the dilemma of religious plurality by direct experience.

His eminent disciple Swami Vivekananda (1863-1902) wrote Practical Adventism (non-Duality), which looks towards all mankind as one's own soul, was never developed among the Hindus universally. I am firmly persuaded that without the help of practical Islam, theories of Vedantism, however fine and wonderful they may be, are entirely valueless to the vast mass of mankind. For our own motherland, a junction of the two systems Hinduism and Islam is the only hope."

If the Maxims:

- No peace among the nations, without peace among the religions.
- No peace among the religions, without dialogue between religions.
- No Dialogue between religions, without investigation of the foundation of the religions.

One needs to study the foundation of all religions, not only without prejudice and bias but also free from preconceived ideas which could overtly our covertly lead to pre-judgment. Misinformation and disinformation would result in misconception, one should carefully verify the source of information and find out whether the information came from reliable or credible origin. It would be needless to say that anyone alleging that other religions are false or labeling the adherents of other religions as Heathens or Kafirs would render the dialogue as counterproductive. It would be equally counter productive to brand any religion, be it Abrahamic or not, to be doctrinally intolerant and consist exhortation for religious violence or it's teaching to be not ecologically friendly.

I would now like to present some points regarding tolerance from Islamic context. Islamic teaching goes beyond tolerance and welcomes the other and celebrates diversity. Allow me to quote some Quranic Verses in support of this view.

Origin Of Human O mankind, fear your Lord, who created you from one soul and created from it its mate and dispersed from both of them many men and women. And fear Allah, through whom you ask one another, and the wombs. Indeed Allah is ever, over you, an Observer. (4:1)

O mankind, indeed We have created you from male and female and made you peoples and tribes that you may know one another. Indeed, the most noble of you in the sight of Allah is the most righteous of you. Indeed, Allah is Knowing and Acquainted. (49:13)

Truth is One

And We have already sent messengers before you. Among them are those [whose stories] We have related to you, and among them are those [whose stories] We have not related to you. And it was not for any messenger to bring a sign [or verse] except by permission of Allah. So when the command of Allah comes, it will be concluded in truth, and the falsifiers will thereupon lose [all]. (40:78)

He has ordained for you of religion what He enjoined upon Noah and that which We have revealed to you, [O Muhammad], and what We enjoined upon Abraham and Moses and Jesus—to establish the religion and not be divided therein. Difficult for those who associate others with Allah is that to which you invite them. Allah chooses for Himself whom He wills and guides to Himself whoever turns back [to Him]. (42:13)

And We have revealed to you, [O Muhammad], the Book in truth, confirming that which preceded it of the Scripture and as a criterion over it. So judge between them by what Allah has revealed and do not follow their inclinations away from what has come to you of the truth. To each of you We prescribed a law and a method. Had Allah willed, He would have made you one nation [united in religion], but [He intended] to test you in what He has given you; so race to [all that is] good. To Allah is your return all together, and He will [then] inform you concerning that over which you used to differ. (5:48)

Say, [O believers], "We have believed in Allah and what has been revealed to us and what has been revealed to Abraham and Ishmael and Isaac and Jacob and the Descendants and what was given to Moses and Jesus and what was given to the prophets from their Lord. We make no distinction between any of them, and we are Muslims [in submission] to Him." (2:136)

Conversion

There is no concept of conversion in Islam. Therefore there is no missionary activity or proselytizing agenda in Islam. Muslims are urged to invite towards the way of truth with wisdom and fair preaching. It is the right of the person who has been invited to accept it or reject it. There is no compulsion in religion and freedom of choice is fully guaranteed in the invitation of Islam.

Invite to the way of your Lord with wisdom and good instruction, and argue with them in a way that is best. Indeed, your Lord is most knowing of who has strayed from His way, and He is most knowing of who is [rightly] guided. (16:125)

And whoever has disbelieved—let not his disbelief grieve you. To Us is their return, and We will inform them of what they did. Indeed, Allah is Knowing of that within the breasts. (31:23)

So remind, [O Muhammad]; you are only a reminder. (88:21)

And obey Allah and obey the Messenger and beware. And if you turn away—then know that upon Our Messenger is only [the responsibility for] clear notification. (5:92)

Tolerance

For you is your religion, and for me is my religion. (109: 6)

O you who have believed, be persistently standing firm for Allah, witnesses in justice, and do not let the hatred of a people prevent you from being just. Be just; that is nearer to righteousness. And fear Allah; indeed, Allah is Acquainted with what you do. (5:8)

And not equal are the good deed and the bad. Repel [evil] by that [deed] which is better; and thereupon the one whom between you and him is enmity [will become] as though he was a devoted friend. (41:34)

Throughout Islamic history, Buddhists—together with Hindus and Zoroastrians, not to mention other religious groups—were regarded by Muslims not as pagans, polytheists, or atheists, but as followers of an authentic religion, and thus to be granted official *dhimmī* status. One of the earliest and most decisive encounters between Islam and Buddhism on the soil of India took place during the short but successful campaign of the young Umayyad general, Muhammad b. Qāsim in Sind, launched in 711. During the conquest of this predominantly Buddhist province, he received petitions from the indigenous Buddhists and Hindus in the important city of Brahmanabad regarding the restoration of their temples and the upholding of their religious rights generally.

He consulted his superior, the governor of Kufa, Hajjāj b. Yūsuf, who in turn consulted his religious scholars. Hajjāj wrote to Muhammad b. Qāsim a letter which was translated into what became known as the 'Brahmanabad settlement'. The request of the chiefs of Brahmanabad about the building of Budh and other temples, and toleration in religious matters, is just and reasonable. I do not see what further rights we can have over them beyond the usual tax. They have paid homage to us and have undertaken to pay the fixed tribute [jizya] to the Caliph. Because they have become dhimmîs we have no right whatsoever to interfere in their lives and property. Do permit them to follow their own religion. No one should prevent them. In the same historian's work, that when Muhammad b. Qāsim died, 'The people of India wept at the death of Muhammad, and made an image of him at Kīraj's.'

(*Ref: Common Ground Between Islam & Buddhism by Reza Shah Kazemi*)

Self-defense and No Aggression

Allah does not forbid you from those who do not fight you because of religion and do not expel you from your homes—from being righteous toward them and acting justly toward them. Indeed, Allah loves those who act justly. (60:8)

Fight in the way of Allah those who fight you but do not transgress. Indeed. Allah does not like transgressors. (2:190)

Dialogue

Say, "O People of the Scripture, come to a word that is equitable between us and you—that we will not worship except Allah and not associate anything with Him and not take one another as lords instead of Allah." But if they turn away, then say, "Bear witness that we are Muslims [submitting to Him]." (3:64)

And do not argue with the People of the Scripture except in a way that is best, except for those who commit injustice among them, and say, "We believe in that which has been revealed to us and revealed to you. And our God and your God is one; and we are Muslims [in submission] to Him." (29:46)

Nothing is said to you, [O Muhammad], except what was already said to the messengers before you. Indeed, your Lord is a possessor of forgiveness and a possessor of painful penalty. (41:43)

Man and its Environment

Islam teaches us that the divine spark is inherit inside physical matter, plants, animals and man. The best of creation "Man" is entrusted with the task of preserving the entire creation. In fact man is sent to this world as a representative of ALMIGHTY to beautify it.

And [mention, O Muhammad], when your Lord said to the angels,

"Indeed, I will make upon the earth a successive authority." They said, "Will You place upon it one who causes corruption therein and sheds blood, while we declare Your praise and sanctify You?" Allah said, "Indeed, I know that which you do not know." (2:30)

And cause not corruption upon the earth after its reformation. And invoke Him in fear and aspiration. Indeed, the mercy of Allah is near to the doers of good. (7:56)

And to [the people of] Madyan [We sent] their brother Shu'ayb. He said, "O my people, worship Allah; you have no deity other than Him. There has come to you clear evidence from your Lord. So fulfill the measure and weight and do not deprive people of their due and cause not corruption upon the earth after its reformation. That is better for you, if you should be believers." (7:85)

And O my people, give full measure and weight in justice and do not deprive the people of their due and do not commit abuse on the earth, spreading corruption. (11:85)

The Holy Prophet declared:

> "The world is beautiful and verdant, and verily Allah, be exalted has made you his stewards in it, and he sees how you acquire yourselves." (Sahee Muslim)
>
> "If any Muslim plants a tree or sow a field, and a human, bird or animal eats from it, it shall be reckoned as charity for him." (Shaee Al-Bukari, Muslim)
>
> "If the day of resurrection comes upon any one of you while he has a seedling in hand let him plant it." (Shaee Al-Bukari)
>
> "Partake of it gladly, so long as you are a benefactor, not a despoiler, a cultivator, not a destroyer."

Conclusion

In order to get rid of bigotries and intolerance that are throwing the planet earth that we all share into an uproar, sincere efforts should be exerted to understand each other's beliefs. We should always bear in mind that there is the other side of the same coin. Accept diversity as a strength and never as a threat. There is dignity in difference and others should be regarded as brothers, regardless of their caste, color, creed or race. It is my solemn belief that if the above principles are adhered to, we would all be able to convert the following:

- Curative conflict resolution to preventive conflict avoidance.
- State environmental regulations to Mass Ecological.
- Consciousness Dialogue-Evasive ideology to Dialogue friendly insight wisdom.

(Al-Haj U Aye Lwin is Chief Convener, The Islamic Centre of Myanmar and Founder and Core Member of Religions For Peace, Myanmar)

10

BHIKKHUNI DHAMMANANDA

BUDDHISM is one religion that talks about peace, and emphasizes that peace is not only in the level of speech but a true Buddhist should live it. It is, therefore most appropriate that at this august gathering we come together to share our idea and our spiritual goal discussing not about peace alone, but about how to heal the world with the teaching from our respective religions.

Being the only Theravada bhikkhuni in this gathering, I have to make sure that I do not cause any conflict of ideas, conflicts which might arise from an attitude either of acceptance or denial. Because if there are two opposing attitudes, then of course, conflict will arise.

To ease the audience from this burden, I would like to briefly explain my position as a Theravada bhikkhuni. Of course, you will agree with me that when the Buddha allowed women to join the Sangha, there was no Theravada yet.

The ordination of Theravada bhikkhunis which has been generally accepted in contemporary world began only in 1998 with the ordination organized by Fo Guang Shan in Bodh Gaya, India. First Fo Guang Shan bhikkhuni and bhikkhu sangha gave ordination to the candidates under the Vinaya tradition of Dhammagupta.

But this ordination viewed from Theravada is not acceptable as it is not Theravada Vinaya. Therefore the most senior Theravada bhikkhus from Sri lanka who attended the ordination ceremony took the 20 newly ordained Sri Lanka bhikkhunis to Sarnath, and gave them yet another ordination. This time within Sima consecrated in Theravada tradition and the 10 most senior

Theravada bhikkhus performed sanghakamma and admitted the bhikkhunis in Theravada tradition.

This was done according the very first allowance given by the Buddha (Cullavagga, Vinaya Pitaka).

Having cleared the air, I hope that our verable bhikkhus present can feel at ease to have a Theravada bhikkhuni among you.

Let me now progress with the topic of Conflict Avoidance.

Buddhism is very rich with meditation techniques, the Buddha prescribed not less than 46 different techniques for our mental training. This itself is a statement of conflict avoidance, that is to accept the difference among individuals. There is no one prescribed mental technique for all. Buddhism respect differences of individuals, this is the beauty of Buddhism.

That technique which works for Mr. A may not work for Mr. B. In this case we have to understand that the masters of old have access to many techniques, and when they take in disciples, the masters usually take time to observe each of the disciple behavior, inclination, temperament, etc. Only then the master will prescribe certain technique to suit the person.

At present, the public do not have the time to come and stay with the master, so that the master could observe him or her. Therefore the meditation technique given is usually for general, does not have a specific answer to each person. Thus, we hear of complaint that the practitioners do not see any progress in their practice.

Another problem also, there is very limited number of masters who would be familiar with various techniques of mental training. Each master tends to teach or instruct only the technique that he knows, which again may not be suitable to that particular student.

To avoid conflict by meditation, sometimes it does not help because of this limitation.

When we focus on conflict avoidance, we need to have time to observe the cause of conflict. Dukkha cannot be removed if we cannot identify Samudaya (cause of it). Some conflicts may be more complicated, there might be layers of causes under what we see at the observable level. Just to give you an example, when the Thais talk about the price of rubber in the market, the very root of it is politics. This is how complicated it could get.

The conflict that we can handle directly is the conflict that is caused within ourselves. Generally, and more often than not, holding on to Atta is the real cause of it expressed through the three brothers who work hand in hand, namely anger, greed and delusion.

Because of the deluded mind we have greed and greed further leads to anger when we do not get what we want. Becoming angry at a person or persons who obstruct us from getting what we want. Because of our deluded mind, we believe in our power to control, and when the opposite do not allow to be controlled, then we are angry. This anger chooses to express itself in the degree according to the power that we think we have.

With application of meditation techniques, one can actually start looking from within, to realize that all the time that we are angry at Mr. A, Mr. A is leading a normal peaceful life, while we ourselves are burning with anger and hatred. The meditation technique that could be apply in this case is either to realize the cause of anger, or to develop metta (loving kindness) first to ourselves and realize that the person whom we are angry with also needs the same loving kindness.

Even meditation technique of looking simply at our breathe can bring wisdom to us.

This breathing in and out, it depends on each other, it does not have its own essence. It cannot depend on itself. When there is breathing in, there must be breathing out. There is duality in our breathe. Buddhism teaches us further that when it has no real existence in itself then it falls into the three characteristics that is anicca (impermanent), dukkha (cannot stay) and anatta (no real self).

With this understanding it allows a person to let go of anger when the reality in a higher level of understanding is applied.

Another technique of handling anger is to put oneself in the situation of the person whom we are dealing with. As soon as we start to look at the conflicting issue from their point of view, and not always from our point of view. We can some how handle the situation better. We slowly reduce our anger and are more willing to compromise to come to a better agreement which will bring about win-win situation.

We also remind ourselves that if we aim at winning all the time, we have to realize that if we win, then it would imply that the opposite party will have to lose. They will not give up, so the conflict is not completely solved. Sometimes that which we now consider our winning could be the cause for further conflict.

But if from the beginning we look at the situation in a Buddhist way it will allow both sides to come to compromise, win some and lose some. But this technique will not cause a remorse feeling in any party. It can be accepted by both parties.

In handling conflict, we have to always find the solution not only for our side but also for their side. If we cannot think for the benefit of others, then we cannot truly solve the conflict.

(Dr. Chatsumarn Kabilsingh, ordained Dhammananda Bhikkhuni, is a Theravādin bhikkuni (Buddhist nun) and serves as the absess of the only temple in Thailand)

11

DHAMMAPIYA

TODAY'S living world seems to be missing something and losing its position, of peace and Harmony. Where has the process of peace and harmony gone? Once Albert Einstein said, "To live in the world is too dangerous". This is a cautious statement because the world has been facing many conditions which are threatening it ever since. Thus world leaders meet in different locations every now and then to speak for the virtue of Peace and Harmony.

The world leaders precisely talk a lot about the global conflicts and its crisis. They do research for the issues in order to get a better way of solution. However, conflicts and problems are getting more and more. In this regard, it is believed that the solution is probably related to a more political approach rather than the combination of spiritual approach. This means that the so-called peace-makers ignore the spiritual power which is able to develop inner peace. Yet political leaders target the consequence of conflicts using theoretical method and they themselves have lost the peaceful mind power for the time being. Therefore, though they are searching for a solution to engage, conflicts are increasing.

According to Buddhism, conflicts arise as a consequence of not of a single cause, but many causes. Many people inside Myanmar and abroad think that conflicts in Myanmar arise frequently because of poverty. That means the people in country are financially poor. But this reasoning is only partially true. This is because poverty doesn't mean only financial poverty but also other kinds, such as educational poverty, and moral and spiritual poverty. Therefore, it is believed that so long as the people do not maintain their moral and spiritual virtues, there is no way to get inner peace. Therefore, it is necessary for the leaders to make efforts for peace building by means of providing spiritual support.

Buddhists introduce the way of solution to the world through a theoretical approach as well as through way of meditation. They state that "no single cause can produce an effect, nor does only one effect arise from a given cause. Rather, there is always a collection of conditions giving rise to a collection of effects"[1] Moreover, Lord Buddha said that main cause of consequences are ignorance (lack of wisdom) and craving which arises from attachment to living world in accordance with *Paticcasamuppāda.* (Dependent Arising)[2].

Today's living people are mostly supporting hedonism. Their life styles are beyond satisfaction and they enjoy themselves with pleasure, power, and sexual activities etc. Therefore, in many conditions they have lost control of the mind and have to face unnecessary fear as well. They feel that their lives are not safe and their surroundings are vulnerable to many conditions. Therefore, it is recalled what Albert Einstein said, "The world is too dangerous to live in, not because of the people who do evil, but because of the people who sit and let it happen." It means that some of the most evil people are those who just sit around and do nothing and there are bad people in the world standing around and complaining a lot without going to fix anything.[3] What **Einstein said is true.**

Nowadays world leaders and religious leaders everywhere attempt to solve the world's global conflicts that are very much dependent on unsolvable conditions. We can see some issues of personal identity, but we cannot see some conflicts and its identity inclusively. That is why though they try to solve the problems by means of using a certain method as well as the political power, to solve problems and conflicts are beyond what they think.

In reality, more than ever our living, the world engages political conflicts rather than religious conflicts. Many people presume that religion is a fundamental cause to introduce the conflicts into the nations. I don't agree to this because many people nowadays fail to sustain their moral and spiritual power. Consequently, there is more conflicts in every nation.

In order to reduce conflicts, it is necessary for political leaders and religious leaders to assume an important role for the nation to get more peace and harmony. This is because the government has political power to authorize the nation to solve such kinds of issues. Otherwise, citizens will take advantages demanding in many conditions—human rights, equal opportunity, justice, freedom of speech, freedom of religion, minority right and so on.

Indeed, the government needs not to take any side and pay attention to maintain the cultural value, historical value and moral conducts. Otherwise, there will be increased conflicts. Therefore, it is necessary to educate citizens to have the ability to know how to manage the country. Otherwise, the country will have to face more problems every now and then.

In Buddhism, people realize that "hatred never ceases through hatred in this world, but through universal love it can be ceased. This is a natural law."[4] Therefore, the world leaders are not supposed to use the political method that targets only conflicts.

We are longing for world leaders as well as religious leaders to develop more spiritual power and great compassion towards the living nations to get more peace and harmony that everyone is longing for. In conclusion, I do believe that this Interfaith dialogue for Peace and Harmony and security will bring blessings to all nations.

(Dr Dhammapiya is Professor at International Theravada Buddhist Missionary University, Yangon)

REFERENCES

1 Bhikkhu Bodhi's translation. *A Comprehensive Manual of Abhidhamma.* (Kuala Lumpur, Malaysia: Selangor Buddhist Vipassana Meditation Society (SBVMS), 2006), 295.

2 Ibid, 294.

3 This quotation is from https://prezi.com.

4 Dhammapada Pāli, verse 5, (Rangon, Burma: Department of Religious affairs, 1972), 14.

Environment Consciousness for a Sustainable World

1

Nirmalanandanatha Mahaswami

NATURE is an integral component in many religious doctrines. It often plays a symbolic role, alongside a pragmatic one. A means to experience the divine, as well as to survive in an often harsh environment. For instance, in any religion or faith that evolved under conditions of severe water scarcity, the holy text offers many prescriptions of water usage and conservation. Water is viewed both as a physical purifier and a moral one.

A radical change in our relationship with nature is no longer just an option. It is a matter of survival. We cannot destroy nature without destroying ourselves. Today, we live in a time of great crisis, confronted by the gravest challenge that humanity has ever faced. The ecological consequences of our own collective actions are our challenges and any tradition understands that man is not separate from nature.

Hinduism is very concerned with the relationship between humanity and the environment. Karma teaches that resources in the world become scarce because people use them for their own ends. Knowing this, Hindus strive for ahimsa, to minimize the harm we cause through our actions in our ordinary, day-to-day lives. As Hindus we revere all life, human, non-human, plant, and animal.

From a Buddhist perspective, a sane and sustainable economy would be governed by the principle of sufficiency: the key to happiness is contentment rather than an ever-increasing abundance of goods. The compulsion to consume more and more is an expression of craving, the very thing the Buddha pinpointed as the root cause of suffering.

Hindus and Buddhists still know we must do all that is humanly possible to protect the Earth and her resources for the present as well as future generations, leading to sustainability.

(Dr. Nirmalanandanatha Mahaswami is the 72nd Pontiff of Sri Adichunchanagiri Mahasamsthana Math, Karnataka, India.)

2

KIREN RIJIJU

I am extremely delighted to participate in this Conference on "Conflict Avoidance & Environment Consciousness" jointly organized by VIF, New Delhi, Sitagu International Buddhist Academy (SIBA), Yangon and the Japan Foundation in collaboration with Myanmar Institute of Strategic and International Studies (MISIS), Yangon, as a follow up to the previous Conferences i.e., Hindu Buddhist Global Initiative for Conflict Avoidance and Environment Consciousness (SAMVAD I) held in New Delhi in September 2015 and the Symposium on "Asian values and Democracy" held at Tokyo in January, 2016, and on both the occasions I participated. I am confident that this conference would further deepen our understanding of shared legacy and different facets of Asian values and also help in creating alternative strategy to the problems of conflict which threaten the peace and stability in the world.

I congratulate the Organizers for this extremely important conference which focuses on environment consciousness and how to expand it in a world more and more concerned with self than with the environment. Conflict Avoidance is other facet of this conference which again is an important ingredient for harmonious co-existence of all human kind, especially in times when individuals and nations are treading on the dangerous lines of insecurity and distrust, with or without any apparent cause.

I am also thankful to Government of Myanmar for their wholehearted support in hosting this conference. India-Myanmar relations are rooted in shared historical, ethnic, cultural and religious ties. As the land of Lord Buddha, India is a country of pilgrimage for the people of Myanmar. India and Myanmar relations have stood the test of time. The geographical proximity of the two countries has helped develop and sustain cordial relations and facilitated people-to-people contact. India and Myanmar share a long land border of over 1600 km and a maritime boundary in the Bay of Bengal. A large population of Indian origin (according to some estimates about 2.5 million) lives in Myanmar. India and Myanmar signed a Treaty of Friendship in 1951. I am confident that such cultural exchanges will further strengthen our bonds.

Talking on the issue of "Environment Consciousness", it would not be out of place to see that for the last two millennia, human beings never faced a truly serious threat to their existence. However, in the third millennium, the ever-deepening global environment crisis poses a real threat of human extinction. Many scientists claim that we have entered a new geological epoch called the Anthropocene which implies a new reality that signifies irreversible changes in the Earth's ecosystems. Together, environmental problems such as the greenhouse effect, marine pollution and destruction of forests are expanding in scale and growing more serious in nature.

And who is responsible for this state of affairs? We are. Today it is hard to find a place on earth that remains unaltered by human needs. In the West, the inherited framework for morality is based on individual rights and entitlements that place human interests at the summit of ethical concerns. However, Eastern religions have much to offer in our quest for answers to the environmental crisis. It is perhaps the Eastern religion that is most associated with ideas of holism and a romantic, pre-modern understanding of nature as a source of spiritual fulfillment.

Our ancient traditions do not make the big distinction found in the "West" between "Nature" and human beings. We do not consider ourselves apart from nature but that we are a part of it. Because humans are tied with nature, damage done upon the earth is also harm done to humans. In the theory of Karma, the effects of our action are in proportion to the greed and hatred which motivated them. As our damage to the planet though stripping of its resources and polluting was motivated by greed, we are now beginning to experience the effects of the greed. The earth is our mirror.

Practice of the First Precept requires respect for all sentient beings not merely humans. This also means respect for all animals. Our relationship with the environment goes much deeper. In Buddhism and Hinduism, we have the concept of *pancha mahabhoota* and *chatur mahabhoota-akash, vayu, agni, jala* and *prithvi.* These are the main elements in the world and everything in the physical creation is composed of these 5 elements. Any imbalance of these elements leads to problems with individual health as well as health of the entire world and its eco system. In Buddhism 'wisdom of equality of all things' enables people to understand all phenomena in terms of dependent origination and to embrace all existences as equal in their intrinsic value.

Indic culture has its roots in *aranya Sanskriti*—forest culture. So, ecological integrity in the past was not a problem. It is the bottom line of everything else in the biosphere. We cannot imagine life flowering sustainably on earth with ongoing ecological disintegration of the biosphere, which is now precipitating into climate change. Climate related disasters are at an all time high. Global carbon emissions continue to rise. Mankind is struggling with the moral dilemmas of waste and consumption. If we analyze our lifestyles, we could conclude that our ethical system which used to help us to be in the state of ecological integrity-is on the verge of collapse.

We have to decide whether we treat nature as a resource or a set of ecosystem foundations or as an enemy to be conquered or a spiritual home in an interconnected world. Population of the world has crossed 7 billion, of this vast numbers are below poverty line. We in the developing world which have large populations much of who are below poverty line are particularly vulnerable to the vagaries of climate change, erratic rainfall patterns, repeated droughts, rise in temperatures with resultant rise in sea levels and the impact on us. In meeting the challenge of elimination of mass poverty consequences of faulty governance structures and past chaos is still unfolding.

The Earth has already witnessed 5 mass extinctions caused by climate change, intense ice ages, volcanic eruptions and meteorite hit. At the current rate of species loss, we are on the verge of losing our biodiversity on which we depend for our own survival. We also need to carefully consider in advance, the possible effects of scientific-technological innovations on the environment because many a times even those intended to serve human society and desires can bring about the destruction of nature leading to hazardous effects. Global warming due to emission of greenhouse gases is such an example. In such cases we need to design inherent pollution mitigation features.

It is my fervent hope that this conference will lead to engaging members of faith based groups, provide moral authority and offer ethical guidelines from our religious leadership. Ethics are the soul of human living, and environmental ethics is a part of environmental philosophy. A new paradigm of well being, connecting individual to social to global responsibility, needs to be framed where human rights are based on rights of nature and both are in the state of 'dependent origination'. In short, the community needs to be motivated to support sustainability practices.

I look forward to the churning of ideas between venerable religious leaders and erudite scholars and hope it will result in giving directions to meet this challenge that threatens the existence of our planet.

(Mr Kiren Rijiju was Minister of State for Home Affairs, Govt. of India from 2014-19)

3

Drikung Kyabgon Chetsang Rinpoche

DURING the last century, in the name of modernisation and development, we lost sight of many issues concerning protection of the environment and wildlife, sustainable development, and the empowerment of local communities in the face of global problems. In addition, globalisation has started to erase unique cultural traditions that have existed for centuries. As we lose these traditions, we are losing skills that allow us to live in harmony with the environment and in peace with other people. This meeting is a wonderful opportunity to dialogue about questions that are critical to our world's future. With the creativity of the human mind and the rich traditions transmitted by different religions, we can bring about sustainable development that allows human beings to flourish in their natural environment.

More than two thousand years ago, two of the Buddha's disciples had a dialogue at Rajghir in India called the Rice Shoot *Sutra (Shalistamba Sutra)*. In this *sutra*, Shariputra tells Maitreya that whoever understands interdependent origination has understood the *Dharma,* and whoever understands the *Dharma* has seen the Buddha. He defines interdependent origination as, "If you have this one thing, that other thing will arise. This one thing arises due to the arising of that other thing." In the *sutra*, the concept of interdependent origination is used to explain the twelve links of interdependent origination

Buddhists apply the concept of interdependent origination to everything in our world, but I believe it is especially useful for thinking about ecology and the relationship between local communities and their natural environment. For instance, the plants and animals in an ecosystem are all dependent on each other. The increase or extinction of a single species affects the entire ecosystem.

An authentic environmental consciousness will develop naturally once people recognize the deep interdependence between humans, plants, and animals. Thus, the ancient Buddhist philosophy of interdependence is critical to the future of our planet, and I believe we must focus our efforts on educating local communites, especially young people, about the power they have to shape the environment they live in.

This is what I have tried to emphasize in my Go Green, Go Organic campaign. Since 2014, I have been working to protect the environment and to raise environmental consciousness among people around the world, especially in the Himalayan region of Ladakh.

We have planted more than two hundred thousand trees in an effort to prevent erosion and give the local people natural resources to harvest sustainably. We have selected several different tree species, including sea buckthorn and fruit trees. This project is aimed at developing sustainable economic opportunities for the local communities.

In addition to planting trees, our main focus is on saving water. The glaciers of the Himalayan snow mountains are melting due to global warming. In the last 30 years, 50 per cent of the glaciers have disappeared. If another 30 years pass without any changes, at lest another 50 per cent will disappear. So this is a very serious issue. There are a dozen major rivers that rise in the Himalayas and bring water to billions of people living downstream, including right here in Myanmar. What will all these people do without drinking water and water for their fields?

We are working on several projects to capture and better harness Ladakh's freshwater resources. In the winter, ice stupa... [explain here]

To capture water in the summer, we are digging trenches that distribute water across a wider area. This reduces erosion and has led an increase in all sorts of wild plants. In the project area, we have even discovered some plants that the local people had never seen before. These plants form a habitat that supports all sorts of life—not just domestic animals, but also wild animals, birds, and even insects. In addition, the oxygen produced by the plants nourishes the entire planet. So this truly benefits all sentient beings.

There is one more point I would like to make. All over the world, economic development has led to great changes in people's lifestyles, and this has impacted the local environment. Today, the tourist industry is booming, especially in Asia, but it brings with it vast amounts of garbage. Earlier this year I traveled to some areas in Indonesia, Vietnam, and Thailand. I saw people on boats throwing trash straight into the ocean. There is now trash all over our planet. This issue is very important for everyone, whether we are talking about highland river systems or ocean islands. In my opinion, the companies and industries that create the garbage (or pollution) should be responsible for cleaning it up.

Finally, we need to develop a broader perspective of the earth as a whole. We need a view that includes all the living beings in this world, even insects. One could say that nature itself is calling for the cooperation of people of all nations and religions. Natural disasters and ecological problems do not choose people of one religion or one nation—contaminated waters flow and poison all, Buddhists and Hindus, Christians and Muslims. So we must create a new level of environmental awareness from the global scale all the way down to local communities. Because environmental issues are global, they cannot be solved by a single organization. I welcome interfaith dialogues and efforts to promote the ecological traditions of different religions.

With this dialogue for peace and harmony, I look forward to achieving a worldwide awareness of our global interdependence and widespread environmental consciousness. And I voice my appreciation of the tireless efforts of individuals, communities, organisations, and governments in arranging this Dialogue for Peace, Harmony and Security.

May there be peace on earth.

(His Holiness the Drikung Kyabgon Chetsang is the Head of the Drikung Kagyu Lineage of Tibetan Buddhism)

4

BARBARA MAAS

What Do We All have in Common?

In 1973, German psychologist Erich Fromm coined the term "**biophilia**" to describe "the passionate love of life and of all that is alive." A decade later, American biologist Edward O. Wilson defined biophilia in his book of the same title as "the urge to affiliate with other forms of life."

The idea resonates with the concepts of universal interconnectedness, reverence for life, and *metta* or loving-kindness, which are at the center of Buddhist philosophy. I believe that embracing and integrating these ideas into our lives provides the solution to the most serious crisis ever faced by life on Earth, as the frantic scramble for power, identity, and resources that grips our increasingly crowded, consumerist, dog-eat-dog society drowns out our sense of interconnectedness and affinity with each other and the natural world.

The 200,000-year history of human colonization of this world has resulted in the most dramatic planetary takeover since life began. Initially, our limited numbers largely diluted our impact on the planet's diversity of life. When the Buddha was born in 623 BCE, the Earth was home to approximately 154 million people. We crossed the 1 billion mark sometime in the early 19th century, and in the course of my lifetime alone the population has risen from 3 billion people in 1960 to more than 7.5 billion today. Human population is projected to reach 9.8 billion by 2050 and 11.2 billion by 2100.

The sheer onslaught of human population growth and associated consumption has simply outstripped the planet's biocapacity. Earth's ecosystems are like a bank account; if what you take out exceeds what goes back in, you're heading for bankruptcy. Earth Overshoot Day (EOD) marks the annual date when humanity has used more from nature than nature can regenerate that year. Since it was first calculated in 1971, this date has crept steadily backwards by nearly five months, indicating that the entire planet is in a deepening ecological deficit. This year EOD fell on 2 August.

Humanity's impact on the Earth is now so profound that experts refer to the current geological epoch as the Anthropocene—the age of man. It is defined by nuclear tests, plastic pollution, mass livestock production, and the degradation of the entire global ecosystem that all organisms, including humans, depend on for air, water, food, and shelter.

Manifestations of Climate Change

- Higher overall rainfall
- Increased risk of drought
- More flooding from storms
- Rising sea levels
- More frequent extreme weather events
- Freshwater shortages
- Mass migrations
- Agricultural productivity loss
- More deaths from floods, storms, heat waves and droughts
- Plant and animal extinctions
- Increases in malaria, food- and water-borne disease and malnutrition
- Ocean acidification
- Social conflict over access to resources

What's New in Climate Change?

- Methane craters in Siberia
- ARCTIC sea ice sank to a record low wintertime extent for the third year in January 2017.
- ANTARCTICA: Larsen C Ice Shelf detaches on 12 July 2017

As human populations grow, so does their impact on the environment. Humans are now the primary driver of species extinction. We have dialed up the rate at which species are disappearing to around 1,000 times that of natural extinction rates. As if that wasn't terrifying enough, the speed of species loss is expected to be 10,000 times higher in the future, affecting countless terrestrial, marine, and freshwater species. Large-bodied animals are particularly at risk, either because they are in our way or because we like to eat them or their body parts.

Thus, we have set over 60 percent of all large herbivores, such as rhinos, elephants, giraffes, and hippos, and three quarters of large predators who depend on large herbivores, e.g., lions, tigers, wolves, and leopards, on a course to oblivion. Their loss will have far-reaching and unexpected downstream effects on other species, the structure of their habitats, and ecological processes. One in four mammal species are threatened with extinction, as are 42 percent of amphibians, all marine turtles, nearly half of all crocodiles, a third of all cacti and conifers, 60 percent of turtles and tortoises, and over 30 percent of reef-forming corals, sharks and rays, and freshwater crabs and crayfish, to name a few.

Each species lost means that a unique strand in the web of life and the result of 4 billion years of evolution is gone for good. There are no winners in this global game of ecological Jenga, as each species' loss brings all of us one step closer to global ecosystem collapse. "*The services and economic value that species provide are irreplaceable and essential to our well-being. Unless we live within the limits set by nature, and manage our natural resources sustainably, more and more species will be driven towards extinction. If we ignore our responsibility we will compromise our own survival.*" said Dr. Jane Smart, director of the IUCN Global Species Programme.

When Sean Maxwell and colleagues analyzed the threats to the 8,688 threatened species currently on the IUCN Red List of Threatened Species, they found that regardless of the threat category or species group, overexploitation and agriculture had by far the greatest impact.

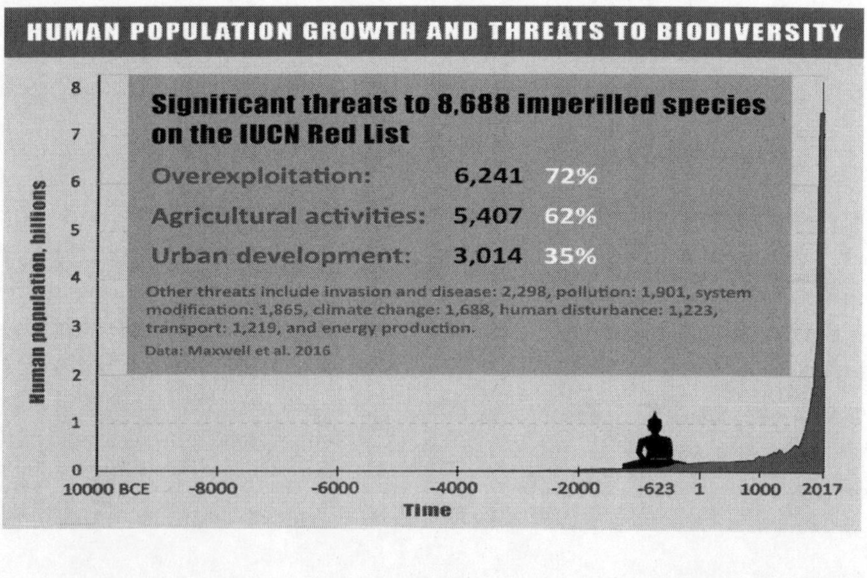

Whether for commerce, recreation, or subsistence, overexploitation imperils 72 percent of species. Rhinos, gorillas, sharks, pangolins, bears, tigers, and elephants are just a few of the more than 2,700 species affected by illegal hunting as a result of market demand for their body parts and meat, or by people plucking them from the wild to be sold as exotic pets.

Overexploitation: Some endangered species can only be found inside protected areas, such as national parks, and even there they are not safe. The surge in wildlife trade in recent years is industrial in scale and largely due to a rise in demand in Asia. According to Interpol, wildlife trafficking is worth US$7–23 billion per year and, together with arms, narcotics, and human trafficking, now ranks among the four most lucrative illicit trade commodities. It is driven by transnational organized crime syndicates that target high-value wildlife without regard for the lives of the animals or people affected. They corrupt local officials, recruit and arm local poachers, create insecurity, and put local communities into a poverty spiral.

Every 15 minutes an elephant is killed for its tusks. Poaching and the illegal trade in ivory have long been the main threats to these majestic animals. In 2010–12, more than 100,000 African elephants were slaughtered—the equivalent of 25 percent of the surviving population of 415,000. At the beginning of the 20th century there were 10 million.

Poaching rhinos for their horns (made from keratin, the same material as human toenails) has also soared in recent years. While its use in traditional Asian medicine persists, rhino horn is increasingly used for display as status symbols, 'party drugs' to relieve hangovers, and for jewelry and other trinkets, or in the tragically mistaken belief that it can enhance male sexual potency. As a result, rhino populations are under siege. Last year, at least 1,342 African rhinos were killed, the highest number since records began. The full horror of the situation becomes clear when we consider that a single 3 gram dose of rhino horn if administered to 3.9 percent of adults in China and Vietnam would require the horn of every last rhino on the planet.

Agricultural activities, including the production of food, fodder, fiber, and fuel crops, as well as livestock farming, aquaculture, and the cultivation of trees, threaten 62 percent of species. A staggering 80 percent of all threatened terrestrial bird and mammal species are being pushed towards extinction by agriculturally driven habitat loss.

The End of Farming?

If current rates of degradation continue, all of the world's top soil could be gone within 60 years. About a third of the world's soil has already been degraded. Generating 3 cm of top soil takes 1,000 years. Main causes of this degradation are chemical-heavy farming techniques, deforestation, and global warming.

The World Food and Agriculture Organization (FAO) estimates that global livestock production accounts for 14.5 percent of the world's greenhouse gas emissions, while the World Watch Institute believes the figure could be as high as 51 percent. Either way, meat and dairy production are the primary contributors of greenhouse gas emissions. Even at lower estimates, livestock production emissions exceed that of the entire transportation sector, which includes cars, trucks, trains, ships, and aircraft.

And it's going to get great deal worse because our *per capita* consumption of meat and dairy products continues to rise. According to the FAO, the human population is predicted to increase by 33 percent by 2050, while demand for meat and livestock products is expected to shoot up by 73 percent by 2050 as a result of growing affluence and urbanization.

We live in a world where the collective mass of the world's livestock animals already exceeds that of wild land mammals by at least 10 times. This upsurge in livestock continues to reduce the availability of grazing and water for wild animals, raises the risk of disease transmission from domestic to wild species, and increases human-wildlife conflict, particularly in the developing world, where livestock production tripled between 1980 and 2002. The extent of the threats I mentioned, as well as many others for which there is no time tight now, is largely determined by growth in human populations and *per capita* income, which drive rising demands for agricultural land and animal protein and their associated threats to biodiversity through habitat destruction and exploitation of wild animal and plant populations.

According to the late Prof. Stephen Hawking, "Now more than at any time in our history, our species needs to work together … we are at the most dangerous moment in the development of humanity."

Part of the environmental harm we are causing is simply the result of our growing numbers. Beyond that, what we consume and in how much quantity determines our impact on the world. This aspect is particularly poignant in world that increasingly seeks fulfillment and happiness through materialism. But as early as 2003, American psychologist Tim Kasser and colleagues found that the more people follow materialistic goals and ambitions, the lower their happiness and life satisfaction, and the fewer pleasant emotions they experience. As materialistic values rise, people also show less concern for the wellbeing of others and are less cooperative, empathic, altruistic and generous. A marked drop in concern for nature is another significant effect of living a materialist lifestyle. In fact, Kasser found that incidences of depression, anxiety and substance abuse too were higher amongst those with consumerist outlook. Small surprise than that consumerism and conspicuous consumption was linked to a fragile sense of self-worth, and on a deep psychological level, was found to serve as a coping strategy for feelings of helplessness and fear of death by providing us with an illusion of power and control. In contrast, a focus on intrinsic values was acted as an effective buffer against materialistic values.

It simply cannot go on like this.

Where Do We Grow From Here?

1. *Children are our future…*

Vegetables! It takes 14 times as much land to produce a ton of beef than to produce the equivalent amount of grain. Put a different way, one acre of land can produce around 250 pounds of beef or 50,000 pounds of tomatoes, up to 53,000 pounds of potatoes or 30,000 pounds of carrots. While it takes around 16,530 liters of water to produce a kilogram of beef, only 1082 liters are required to grow the same amount of potatoes. As water shortages begin to bite around the globe, just one person's decision to give up meat could free up water for 445 people. Moving toward a plant-based diet would therefore slow down climate change and confer significant conservation and humanitarian benefits. Recognizing the far-reaching climate and environmental impacts of meat consumption, China last year announced plans to cut the country's meat consumption by 50 percent. Put bluntly, without making these changes, we will be unable to keep global warming below the dangerous level of 2°C, which was agreed by 196 nations in the 2015 Paris climate accord.

Meat-free eating also provides significant health benefits, including lower blood pressure and cholesterol, as well as a reduced risk of chronic illnesses such as heart disease, colon cancer, and type-2 diabetes. Springmann and colleagues estimate that a plant-based diet could save up to 8 million lives by 2050, lead to healthcare-related savings and could avoid climate-related damages totaling US$1.5 trillion. Perhaps surprisingly, three-quarters of these benefits would occur in developing countries. The researchers estimate the overall economic benefits to be US$1–31 trillion—equivalent to 0.4–13 percent of projected global GDP in 2050.

It is up to us to be the light at the end of this tunnel, but will we be able to use compassion and wisdom to make the changes that are clearly necessary? For many, compassion alone is reason enough to steer clear of meat and animal products. For many more, kindness and common sense stop when it comes to what's on their plate. I grew up in Germany on a traditional German diet dominated by meat and sausages. I also witnessed first-hand the desperate suffering to which we subject domestic animals from the moment they are born to their violent deaths and gave up meat some 30 years ago because I could no longer reconcile my behavior with my conscience. Looking back, this was one of the best decisions I ever made. My only regret is that I waited so long. I am sharing this with you in the hope that it will strengthen your resolve and your belief that you, too, can take this important step towards a natural, healthy and compassionate diet—whether out of kindness toward individual animals or humans, or our planet's life support system as a whole.

More than 70 billion animals are raised for slaughtered every year.

As a Slaugherhouse worker recounted, "My job was to squeeze the coagulated blood down the hole in the floor. The blood was not to exceed more than 3 inches deep. I remember the smell, the uncontrollable shaking and the fearful cries of the cows while they were waiting their turn at death. I know they knew death was near. I remember the Kill Floor team high-fiving each other because they broke the record, killing 107 cows in 1 hour."

In the words of Vietnamese Zen master Thich Nhat Hanh, "We must look deeply. When we buy something or consume something, we may be participating in an act of killing. This precept [non-killing] reflects our determination not to kill, either directly or indirectly, and also to prevent others from killing."

Recognizing that we are at a crucial crossroads, where our survival and that of other species is at stake as a result of human actions, the Buddhist Climate Change Statement urges reduced consumption and the adoption of plant-based diet.

Earlier this year, Buddhist leaders, leading scientists, and scholars met in India to develop practical action plans to address, among other issues, the current environmental crisis. The resulting *Nalanda Declaration on Animals and the Environment* acknowledges the responsibility of the Buddhist community in preventing further species loss and animal suffering through the consumption of wildlife products and meat.

In fact, the Buddha himself encourages us to integrate respect and revere the lives of other beings into our actions. In the *Lankavatara Sutra* he states:

> *"Meat-eating is rejected by me in such sutras as the* Hastikakshya, *the* Mahamegha, *the* Nirvana, *the* Angulimaliya, *and the* Lankavatara. *Meat-eating is forbidden by me everywhere and all the time for those who are abiding in compassion. If, Mahamati, meat is not eaten by anybody for any reason, there will be no destroyer of life. Thus Mahamati, meat-eating I have not permitted to anyone. I do not permit. I will not permit. There may in time to come people who make foolish remarks about meat-eating, saying, "Meat is proper to eat, unobjectionable, and permitted by the Buddha. Meat-eating is medicine; again it is like a child's flesh; follow the proper measure and be averse to meat".*

> Sustainability is a matter of life and death for people on the planet. A sustainable future cannot be achieved without conserving biological diversity - animal and plant species, their habitats and their genes - not only for nature itself, but also for all 7 billion people who depend on it.
>
> *J. Marton-Lefèvre, Former Director General, IUCN*

The World has Changed. Adapt or Die?

If we don't, humanity will end up like this and drag everyone else with them.

Scientists have shown us what the facts are and what needs to be done. But to persuade enough people to act the "Earth needs YOU!". Put it in peoples' heart.

(Dr Barbara Mass is the Head of International Species Conservation for NABU International)

5

ASANGA TILAKRATNE

NATURE AND ENVIRONMENT IN BUDDHIST THOUGHT: A BASIS FOR A HEALTHY ENVIRONMENTAL OUTLOOK

Introduction

'Environment' is a broad term which refers to the surroundings where human beings, animals and plant life exist and interact with one another. An environment needs to be understood in a particular context, in which human beings play an important role. However, the concept of nature often referred to in these types of discussions, has to be understood as having a broader connotation, to include not only human beings, animals and plant life but also the globe as a whole including its rivers, forests, mountains, valleys, plains, deserts and oceans; the sun, moon and stars; and tsunamis, hurricanes, volcanoes, and floods. Some of these phenomena may not be a part of human being's immediate environment.

Although a human being is a part of nature in its broad sense, and at times, a helpless victim of the workings of the larger elements of nature, referred to above, still he occupies a very special place in it, owing to the power of his mind by which he can, to a large extent, determine the matters relating to his own life and the rest of the nature. While this state of affairs places the human being in an advantageous position vis-à-vis the rest of the nature, it poses an ethical and moral challenge for him: he has to determine the right balance between his own existence and that of the nature.

In this study I propose to discuss first, nature as a broad phenomenon encompassing the entire globe and the place and the role of human being in it, as understood in Buddhism. Next I will narrow down the discussion to environment and discuss human beings, animals and plant life, as constituting the environment experienced by human beings.

Human Being and Nature

Nature in its broad sense includes the world with all its conscious and non-conscious elements. In the early discourses of the Buddha, nature in this comprehensive sense is termed '*loka*', which has been used in several related senses. It has been used to refer to: (i) Physical world; (ii) world as extending much beyond the world we live in (universe);[1] (iii) (mainly but not exclusively) all human beings who live in the world;[2] (iv) human being with his physical body, perceptional and cognitive aspects.[3] The first two refer to the spatial dimension of the world whereas the third refers, in a figurative sense, mainly to human beings who live in it. The fourth is the philosophical use of the term. These meanings are inter-woven and hard to distinguish one from another and often overlap. One has to depend heavily on the context to determine, which is which. In this discussion I will not elaborate on these different meanings which have been already studied by many Buddhist scholars. I will examine *loka* as referring to beings occupying the different planes of the universe with the purpose of determining the status of the human being among such beings.

Loka in Buddhist discourses has a broad meaning that extends much beyond the human world and human beings. It is said that the message of the Buddha's first sermon went as far as the highest point of the universe, the *Akanitthaka Brahama* world. It is further said that when the Buddha completed his preaching the 'system of ten thousand worlds' (*dasa sahassi loka dhatu*),[4] it included the idea that there are an infinite number of beings occupying these worlds.

In the well-known threefold analysis of the world, as the world of sensual pleasures (*kama-loka*); fine-material world (*rupa-loka*); and non-material world (*arupa-loka*); the human world comes within the sensual world where it is one among the other four realms, namely, those of animals, and hungry ghosts, and hells and heavens. In these worlds there are many beings with differing material conditions. Those who are born in the animal realm, the realm of hungry ghosts and hells, all live lives full of misery. The latter two groups have long spans of life to suffer. The divine beings have long spans of life to enjoy the fruits of their past good karmas.

The picture of human life is a little more complex. The discourses unanimously say that to be born as a human being is an extremely rare occurrence in one's long samsaric existence. According to the well-known simile of the tortoise blind in one eye, the chances of one being born as a human being are even rarer than the chances of meeting together of the hole of an axel floating in the vast ocean, with the one remaining eye of the tortoise which is roaming equally aimlessly in the vast ocean and being able to see the sky through that hole. Even if one gets such a rare opportunity to be born as a human being, the span of his life is relatively short and the existence is a mix of pleasures and pains.

There are two ways to perceive this state. On the one hand, to be born as a human being with a relatively shorter span of life is considered to be conducive for the realisation of the Dhamma, because to be born in hells with all-pervasive long-lasting suffering, would not allow people to think of anything higher or better. Being born in heavens full of pleasures means that the divine beings do not have any need to seek higher realisation. Even to be born in the realm of Brahmas, as a result of attaining worldly *jhanas* is considered to be a hindrance, on the path of progress. While this is a positive way of perceiving human existence, there is a sense in which human life with its shorter life span, and accompanied miseries is highlighted, as not worthy of being cherished.[5]

This seemingly contradictory position stems from the soteriological urgency found in the teachings of the Buddha. Only the human being is capable of fully realising the Dhamma. Heavens have too many pleasures and hells have too much pain; only human existence has both. In that sense human life is relatively more valuable than that of divine beings, not to mention the inhabitants of hells. From this perspective, human life needs to be placed higher. But if a human being considers his life exclusively as a source of pleasure then he is not likely to follow the path. In order to motivate a human being to follow the path, while laying stress on the value of his life as a human being, the short span of life, with its potential miseries has to be emphasised. The purpose is to create a sense of urgency in a person so that he follows the path 'as if his head is aflame'.[6]

According to Buddhism the world as a natural phenomenon, is independent of human beings. It would exist whether there were human beings or not. While discussing the causally conditioned nature of reality, the Buddha emphasised this aspect of reality in the following words:

> Whether there is an arising of Tathagatas or not arising of Tathagatas, that element still persists, the stableness of the Dhamma, the fixed course of the Dhamma, specific conditionality. A Tathagata awakens to this and breaks through it. Having done so, he explains it, teaches it, proclaims it, establishes it, discloses it, analyses it, elucidates it. And he says: See![7]

In subsequent Buddhist literature[8] this conditionality has been described with reference to the five spheres that include the physical, the psychological and the moral. These include, the occurrence of seasons (*utu-niyama*), plants (*bija-niyama*), moral actions (*kamma-niyama*), phenomena (*dhamma-niyama*) and working of the mind (*citta-niyama*). What is highlighted is that these aspects of the nature function without any agent, human or divine.

The *Agganna-sutta*[9] (Discourse on the Knowledge of Beginning) confirms this way of understanding. According to the sutta, human beings come into a world that was already there. The world evolves through four stages: The stage of continuing expansion (*vivattamaana*); the expanded stage (*vivatta*); the stage of continuing contraction (samvattamaana); and the contracted stage (*samvatta*). They come into this world at the beginning of the expanding stage. The four stages have nothing to do with human beings. In this sense human beings are mere visitors in this world, which has its own way of evolution. The *sutta*, however, records how human beings started gradually interacting with the world, by way of feeding on the earth, demarcating limits of the earth and owning what they demarcated and so on. This suggests that they 'created' their own world from this world, and to that extent we can say that the world and the human beings depend on each other. The story of the *Agganna* is not one of the beginning of the world or the evolution of human beings in it. It is meant to be a moral lesson: It tells the story of the gradual degeneration of human society and proposes ways to regenerate it. But the world goes through its cycle whether or not human beings exist in it, or do whatever they do. The world as matter (*rupa*) is independent of human beings. It keeps on changing endlessly, as a result of which it produces, among others, the eruption of volcanoes and tsunamis caused by the disturbances at the bottom of the earth.

Finally, when the four stages of the cycle are over, the world gets destroyed. According the *Sattasuriyuggamana-sutta*, at the conclusion of the contracted stage, there arise seven suns one after the other. At the rising of the seventh, the entire world, including its human inhabitants, is reduced to ashes. The human being is helpless before these natural phenomena. It is this human helplessness that is articulated in the *Ratthapala-sutta*, as 'the world is devoid of protection, it does not have an overlord (to protect it)—*attaano loko anabhissaro.*

In Buddhist understanding the world is not the creation of an all-powerful God. Neither is the human being such a creation. While the world is subject to natural and physical laws, the human being is subject to his own actions. In the absence of a creator and a purpose, the world is neither moral nor immoral. Although helpless at times, human being is not a totally helpless victim of nature. He can play a creative role by creating his own 'world' within nature. The vastness of nature reminds the human being of his physical limitations. But at the same time by developing the power of mind he can make himself greater, than nature itself. These remarks may be substantiated with reference to the Buddha's words to a disciple who travelled at great speed, in search of the end of the universe. Seeing the disciple engaged in this unending mission, the Buddha called him back and said the following: One can never reach the end of the universe by travelling. Without reaching the end of the universe there will not be a release from suffering.[10]

The first part of this statement refers to the end of the physical universe which is endless, and hence lies beyond human physical capacity. The second part seems to refer to 'universe' in a figurative sense, according to which it is one's own inner universe which has to be penetrated by the wisdom, in order to attain the end of suffering. This particular discourse of the Buddha reveals both human limitations and human potential vis-à-vis nature. In sum, in the Buddhist view, a human being should neither be arrogant nor be servile, but be realistic about his position in nature.

Taking into consideration the above discussion, it is necessary to clarify the position of the human being vis-à-vis nature, according to Buddhism. In theistic religions the superior position of human being is asserted on the basis of his creation by God, who created a human being in his own image. This has been understood as a human-centred world view in which the world (nature) created by God, is left at the disposal of the human being for him to do as he deems fit. This has been understood as leading to the human exploitation of nature, resulting in the destruction of nature and the pollution of the environment. One early analysis of this is by Lynn White (in the paper "The Historical roots of our ecological crisis", published in *Science,* 1967). He describes the world-wide ecological crisis as a problem created by modern science and technology, which is western in origin, guided by the Judeo-

Christian tradition. He specifically refers to the western religious image of man as superior to nature and nature, as created by God, for the use of man. He says:

> What people do about their ecology depends on what they think about themselves in relation to things around them. Human ecology is deeply conditioned by beliefs about our nature and destiny—that is, by religion.

Although a human being's own image about himself may not be the only reason why he exploits nature so relentlessly, it is nonetheless, a powerful rationale for his behaviour. One's attitude toward nature is shaped by one's attitude to oneself. If one's self-image is that of a master, naturally nature becomes the slave. A slave is a mere object at one's hand, a mere means to one's personal ends, not a human being proper. Usually moral reasoning is not considered applicable to anything, other than human agents. In the west it is only recently that they have started thinking that animals are deserving of moral consideration. Renee Descartes, the 16th century French philosopher who is considered the father of modern philosophy, considered animals as 'automata'—some type of machines that are programmed to function—and hence do not come within the purview of moral considerations. Nature in its wider sense including the natural environment was seen as something to be exploited, to be made use of and to be conquered. It is only very recently that this way of thinking has started changing for better. This self-centred attitude, coupled with human beings' endless desire for wealth to be used for sensual gratification, paves the way for exploitation of nature's resources to the maximum possible. The Buddhist position arising from a non-theistic world view, is understood to be conducive for the protection of nature and environment.[11]

Beyond this contrast between theistic religions and non-theistic Buddhism and the subsequent realisation of the relative desirability of Buddhism, there is still a question regarding the Buddhist standpoint on the place of the human being in the nature. Does the Buddhist love for nature and a harmonious existence with nature mean, that at a crucial point the human being should be subordinated to nature? Or to put the same question differently, at a crucial point, which one should be given preference—the human being or nature? Some advocates of ecology seem to think that our ecological thinking has to be completely devoid of any concern for human interests.[12] The question is whether we can think of nature or environment as totally outside of us. Is there any meaning to nature or any discussion on nature [After all in the absence of human beings there will not be any discussion whatsoever!] in the absence of human beings? Any discussion of environment will be out of question without reference to human beings.

If the human being is indispensable in this whole process, what would be the Buddhist outlook toward the interaction between nature and human being? There is no doubt about the Buddhist attitude to individualism which ultimately is a manifestation of a craving that Buddhism considers to the source of suffering. But can an ordinary human being do away with his own sense of individuality in terms of his existence in the world. The Buddhist answer is 'no'. But at the same time Buddhism says, that we have to get rid of our craving, the root cause of individualism. It has to be done gradually like a sailor who has to repair his boat while floating in the sea. This means that so long as the human being is in the world he has to survive by making use of the resources belonging to the world. He has to cut trees to build his houses; build bridges across rivers, build dams for irrigation and generate power, and make tunnels through mountains. Human beings interfere with nature, but Buddhism is not opposed to such activities, to a certain extent. If the human being devastates nature in so doing, then Buddhism would show him that he is endangering his own survival (which is common sense!). But the inescapable fact is that ultimately this environmental love has its roots in individuality!

In this situation, the Buddhist approach will be, to adopt a non-extremist middle position toward nature. It is clear that insects that threaten human life, have to be eliminated. But Buddhism would say that we should endeavour to create an environment in which such harmful insects cannot flourish, so that the issue of terminating them does not arise or will be minimised. Eating meat is another issue which I discuss briefly below. A life on earth without any pain to oneself or the others appears an impossibility. What could be expected according to Buddhism, is a life of minimum pain to oneself and the others. In Buddhist thinking, the two pillars of good human behaviour are compassion (*karuna*) and wisdom (*panna)*, which have to be balanced by each other. In a world of human beings' animals and plants, rivers, mountains, etc. only the human being is capable of moral reasoning. In this sense he is superior to the rest of the nature. This allows the human being to make balanced decisions and above all to transcend oneself individually or collectively. But there is a limit: A human being cannot opt for self-destruction at a crucial event.

Environment: Human Being Toward other Human Beings

In the concept of environment as outlined above, the relationship between human beings is of utmost importance. How he behaves toward the rest of the human society ought to occupy a central place in a human being's environment consciousness. In most cases it constitutes his immediate environment, with which he has emotional and cultural ties. In addition, because of its potential for emotional, intellectual and inner development, a human life is worthy of being preserved and cherished. Buddhism removes the obstacles that stand in the way of happiness, and provides guidance for peaceful and rewarding human relations.

A major factor that prevents human beings from interacting with each other compassionately and rewardingly, are the assumed differences, owing to which some are considered high and the others low. In the Indian context, this was the 'colour phenomenon' (*varna-dharma*) and society was divided into four groups. At the top of the hierarchy were Brahmins (priests) with sudras (slaves) occupying the bottom. The Buddha rejected this hierarchy as baseless and demonstrated through rational argument,[13] that there are no marks that separate one human group from another. In discussing this matter with two Brahmin youths, Vasettha and Bharadvaja, who were of the opinion that they were the highest among the 'colours', the Buddha showed them that there are no different types of human beings, unlike the different types of animals, birds, reptiles and plants. The Buddha pointed out that human beings have no marks on their hair, heads, ears, noses, eyes, lips, brows, shoulders, necks etc. which distinguish one from another human being.[14] Having established this fact, the Buddha concluded his argument in the following words:

> In human bodies in themselves—nothing distinctive can be found.
> Distinction among human beings—Is purely verbal designation.[15]

What is meant by 'verbal designation' (*pannatti*) in this context is that assumed differences among human beings are only a popularly agreed upon convention, which does not refer to anything real. In the Buddhist monastic practice only, seniority is acknowledged as the criterion of recognition. Although inner attainments are valued and those with such attainments are revered, among the Sangha what matters most is the seniority of one's monastic practice. Thus, in Buddhism one is considered higher than others, only on the basis of one's virtues. It is on this same ground that *bhikkhus* and *bhikkhunis* are considered higher than *upasakas* and *upasikas*. The Sangha in this broad sense consists of a community of the followers of the path leading to nirvana, the extinction of suffering. Their inter-relation is characterised by 'mutual advice and mutual up-lifting' (*annamanna vacanena annamanna vutthapanena*[16]).

The role of karma in determining differences among human beings is accepted in the teachings of the Buddha. In the discourse on the shorter exposition of action, the following conversation occurs between the Buddha and the young Brahmin Subha:

> Master Gotama, what is the cause and condition why human beings are seen to be inferior and superior? For people are seen to be short-lived and long-lived, sickly and healthy, ugly and beautiful, uninfluential and influential, poor and wealthy, low-born and high-born, stupid and wise. What is the cause and condition, Master Gotama, why human beings are seen to be inferior and superior?
>
> Student, beings are owners of their actions, heirs of their actions; they originate from their actions, are bound to their actions, have their actions as their refuge. It is action that distinguishes beings as inferior and superior.

In this discussion the Buddha lays much emphasis on karma as the cause and condition of differences among human beings. But depending on what is understood by action in this context, the role attributed to karma may vary greatly. The popular interpretation of karma in this context means karma as the accumulated force behind one's samsaric existence. In this interpretation karma becomes the inescapable to which one has to succumb. If we understand karma in this context, as human action, then the reading can convey a very different emphasis. Karma in this sense is, what is done (or not done) by oneself. According to Buddhism any conscious action produces results in accordance its moral character. As the two first Dhammapada stanzas articulate,[17] what is said or done with a polluted mind produces misery and what is said or done with a purified mind, produces happiness. Buddhism does not consider this process as something done by someone, but as a natural process in which the nature of the action determines the nature of its outcome. This has been described as 'the principle of action' (*kamma-niyaama*) which is one among five such phenomena, which take place depending on causes and conditions.[18]

The idea of human action as one's responsibility, when coupled with the idea of oneness of the humanity, provides a sound basis for a system of social ethics. *Sila* or virtue as the beginning of the path becomes meaningful only in a social context. The five precepts (*panca-sila*): abstaining from killing; stealing; sexual misconduct; lying; and taking intoxicants are basically social virtues. The first four specifically require an outside society as a precondition, for those actions to exist. Abstaining from these misdeeds is tantamount to assuring security to the society. In this manner, *sila* is basically how one should behave toward others.

In addition to this somewhat negative presentation of social morality, there is substantial discussion in Buddhism on how one should behave toward the rest of the society. The *sila* has been described positively as protection of life as opposed to killing, safeguarding others' property as opposed to stealing, being happy and content with one's spouse as against sexual misconduct and speaking what is true, pleasant and meaningful as opposed to telling lies, harsh words and meaningless things. The well-known *Sigalovada-sutta*[19] lists six types of social relations, namely: Parents and children; teachers and students; husbands and wives; friends and friends; masters and servants; and religious people and their lay supporters. It is noteworthy that this classification includes such vulnerable groups as children, women and the elderly and provides adequate provisions for nurturing and protecting them. Although this account does not specifically refer to the disabled, they are naturally provided for, when these social groups are protected.[20] In this same context the *Sigalovada-sutta* refers to the four ways of treating others well, namely: Giving (*dana*), pleasant speech (*peyya vajja*), working for the upliftment of others (*attha-cariya*) and even-handed treatment (*samaanattataa*) and concludes by pointing out that "these things make the world go round like the chariot's axle-pin".

In addition to the inclusion of good friends as an important aspect in one's network of social relations, Buddhism considers the phenomenon of good friend (*kalyana-mitta*) as an indispensable factor for success in anyone's life. Usually the Buddha is described as the good friend of all, for he guides all those who join him in the path of cessation of suffering. For the same reason one's teachers are one's good friends, and the entire society can be a community of good friends. When Ananda said that half the improvement in the religious life is owing to good friends, the Buddha corrected him saying that it was not half, but all the improvement in religious life, was owing to good friends.[21]

The ideal Buddhist social life is characterised by the four states of mind manifested in one's behaviour toward others: Loving kindness (*metta*);

compassion (*karuna*); altruistic joy (*mudita*); and equanimity (*upekkha*) which are described as 'unlimitables' (*appamanna*) by the texts. It is said that the Great Brahma displays these virtues toward all beings, and parents have them toward their own children. The *Karaniya-metta sutta*[22] exemplifies the highest degree of these virtues, when it says that one should practice loving kindness toward all beings, 'as if a mother would protect her only child at the risk of her life.'

Whether a person has these virtues or not, is mainly revealed by one's attitudes and behaviour toward others. How carefully and considerately one drives one's vehicle, how one disposes one's garbage, how one mis/uses common properties such as water and air—all these and many other similar instances, reveal whether or not, one has the above-mentioned qualities. The pollution of air, water and atmosphere is mainly due to the selfishness of people. Being insensitive to nature is not only a wrong way of treating nature but it is also being insensitive to other, fellow human beings. We will discuss our behaviour toward nature shortly, and hence we will refer to nature here only in so far, as it affects others. In this context we can see that how one treats one's fellow human beings and nature, are inter-dependent.

At this point one may ask as to why one should treat other human beings and nature in this manner. Several answers to this may be given from a Buddhist point of view. One response is that human nature is shared by all human beings. Earlier in our discussion with reference to the *Vasettha-sutta* we found that Buddhism lays emphasis on the oneness of all human beings. It goes without saying that all human beings have similar mental and physical feelings and sensations. Supplementing this thinking, the Buddha says that all beings like happiness and dislike unhappiness (*sukha kaama dukkha patikkuula*).[23] If this nature is common to all beings, including human beings, then one should apply this insight to oneself and avoid inflicting pain on others. "All tremble at the rod. All fear death. Comparing others with oneself, one should neither strike nor cause to strike"—the Buddha says.[24] Besides, according to the Buddhist analysis, hatred is at the root of all unskilful (*akusala*) actions[25] which are good neither for oneself, nor for others. Its opposite, friendliness, is therefore good for oneself and others, including, in this context, nature as a whole.

Human Being Toward Animals

As seen above, Buddhism considers all living beings, human beings and animals, as constituting one whole, particularly in respect of the universally shared psychological, emotional and karmic traits. Certain aspects of Buddhist ethical behaviour, such as non-violence, spreading the sentiment of friendliness (*metta,*) are applicable to all living beings. At the same time, however, Buddhism places human beings above other living beings. We need to take into consideration several aspects of the Buddhist teaching and practice in order to understand the Buddhist position accurately.

In the foregoing we noticed that Buddhism has two seemingly contradictory views of human life: On the one hand, it places the human being at a higher position and values human life as a rare opportunity; but on the other hand, it says that human life itself is short and hence should not be taken to be overly valuable. The reason for these two attitudes is the soteriological opportunity and potential for both worldly and inner development that Buddhism sees in human beings. In other words, the Buddha wished human beings to be well aware of their relatively advantageous intellectual position over the animal world, and at the same time, to not waste their life without making proper use of it, for outer as well as inner development, which culminates in ending one's samsaric suffering.

According to Buddhism, animal life is a 'hell', and beings are born as animals, as a result of their bad actions. Human life, on the contrary, is the result of good actions. So this makes human beings naturally higher than animals. So how should they be treated is an interesting question in the Buddhist context.

The Buddhist thinking on the status of animals may be illustrated with reference to the Buddhist monastic law code (*Vinaya*). The highest offence for the Buddhist bhikkhus and bhikkhunis is 'defeat' (*paaraajika*) upon violation of which, they lose the membership in the Sangha, the highest loss according to the *Vinaya.*[26] One among these grave and irreparable offences, is the intentional killing of a human being. Interestingly, killing a non-human (animal) is not included among these offences, but it is included in the minor offences (*pacittiya*), for which the offender may be pardoned, by an act of confession.

The Buddhist attitude to animals is one of loving kindness (*mettaa*). The well known *Karaniyametta-sutta,* referred to above, articulates the scope of this sentiment in the following words:

> Whatsoever living things there are whether they be feeble or strong, without exception, whether long or large, middling, short, minute or massive;

> Whether seen or unseen, or whether they live far or near, whether already come into being or still seeking birth, may all beings be happy at heart.

This very sentiment has been elaborated in the *Ahi Sutta* of the *Anguttara-nikaya*:[27]

> My metta is for those who have no legs, for those who have two legs, four legs, and those who have many legs. ... All beings, all those who have life, all those who are born, may all of them see what is good; may not any evil befall them.

The reason for this treatment, as we saw above, is that all fear death and life is dear to all (*sabbesam jivitam piyam*[28]). Furthermore, it is said by the Buddha that in one's long samsaric journey it is not easy to find a being who was not one's mother, father, brother, sister, son or daughter.[29] This is an added reason, why one should not harm any being including animals.[30]

Before concluding this part of the discussion, it is necessary to address the issue of meat eating. There is no doubt that the Buddhists are against killing (human beings or animals). It is also prohibited for householders to trade in meat. It is one of the five prohibited trades. Although the Buddhist position on killing has been unambiguous the same cannot be said about the issue of meat eating. In the *Vinaya* the Buddha instructs his monastic disciples to eat meat only if they know that it was not killed for them, that nobody told them that it was killed for them and that they did not have any doubt that it was not killed for them (*Vinaya II,* p.197; *Majjhima-nikaya* 55). This is described as 'meat purified at three ends'. The *Amagandha-sutta* (Discourse on Carrion Smell) of the *Sutta-nipata* (239-252) is an indirect defence of the practice of meat eating, in which the Buddha says that what is more important is not the eating of meat but the overall virtuous behaviour. What he says, in other words, is that an otherwise immoral person does not become moral by the mere practice of not eating meat. The *Vinaya* further records that when Devadatta requested the Buddha to make abstaining from partaking of meat, a compulsory rule for the bhikkhus and bhikkhunis, the latter left it to individual discretion. It should also be mentioned that the *Vinaya* refers to proper and improper varieties of meat (*Vinaya* I pp.216-220). These instances make clear that the Buddha did not prohibit his disciples from eating meat provided, they were not directly involved in the killing. The question one tends to ask is: Can you eat animals if you practice *metta* towards them. The *Theravada* answer to which seems to be: one cannot practice *metta* towards dead carcasses, and hence nothing wrong in eating dead carcasses.[31] This discussion could continue and I would like to direct the reader to one of my earlier studies on this issue, for a detailed discussion.[32]

Human Beings and Plant Life

The following statement occurs in the *Jataka*:

> One should not break a branch of a tree under which one sat or rested. [If one did so] he is a villainous traitor.[33]

The *Vinaya* records that for seven days the newly enlightened Buddha kept on looking with gratitude at the Bodhi tree, under which he attained enlightenment. This is a very fascinating sentiment which suggests that trees, and plant life by extension, were regarded by Buddhists as a part of their moral universe. Usually one does not talk about trees and plants, or nature in general, as if they were beings like other living beings, who should be treated as partners in our moral discourse. Jains in ancient India went a step further, when they said that plants have a form of life and thus harming or destroying plant life was considered morally reprehensible. Although the Buddha too asked his monastic followers, to respect this popular sensitivity, cutting a tree was not considered a moral lapse. It was only a part of good monastic behaviour.

In the Theravada Buddhist tradition, we see the Buddha himself and his disciples adoring nature including trees, plants, rivers and mountains. The early monasteries were housed in gardens (*aaraama*) full of trees and plants. This tradition continues even till today and the Buddhist monasteries (in Sri Lanka) are usually called *'arama'*. There is much in the *Vinaya* on the orderliness and cleanliness of the Buddhist monasteries and the safe keeping of the properties of those monasteries, which were meant to be used by all members of the community who came from four directions (*caatuddisa sangha*).[34] Those who have purified themselves of defilements are said to delight in natural beauty. The *Dhammapada* says:

> Delightful are the forests where worldlings delight not; the passionless will rejoice (therein), (for) they seek no sensual pleasures (99).[35]

The *Theragatha* and *Therigatha* (two works in the fifth collection of the *Basket of Discourses*) wherein the joyous memories of both male and female arahants are recorded, bear witness to these enlightened persons' love for nature. This is one aspect of the early Buddhist attitude to nature and environment.

The other is the pragmatic aspect in which the enlightened avail themselves of aspects of nature and environment, without any attachment or aversion. Doctrinally this attitude has been articulated as "having abandoned severe attachment (*abhijjha*) and resentment (*domanassa*) with regard to the world."[36] Even though the context is different, the well known 'simile of the raft' (*kullupama*)[37] exemplifies this attitude. Out of a sense of gratitude, one does not carry on one's back the raft which was useful for crossing a river. The right behaviour toward the raft is to leave it behind on the shore (to be used by others). One makes use of natural resources with least harm to those things, till one lives and then exits gracefully leaving nature and environment as intact as possible, for the sake of others. Here again what is at play are compassion and wisdom, the two pillars upon which human behaviour should be based according to Buddhism.

Concluding Remarks

In this study we have examined the Buddhist attitude to nature and environment mainly as found in the *Theravada* Pali discourses. In the first part of the discussion we examined how Buddhism defines the relation between human beings and nature and the role and status of human being vis-à-vis nature. In particular we argued that the Buddhist attitude to nature or environment cannot be considered, without locating the human being within it. In the rest of the discussion, we studied a human being's attitude to other human beings, animals and plant life, and found that one's overall attitude and behaviour toward nature and environment should be guided by compassion and wisdom.

(Asanga Tilakaratne, PhD is a Professor of Pali and Buddhist Studies at University of Colombo, Sri Lanka)

REFERENCES

(Page reference to Pali texts in footnotes are to Pali Text Society, UK editions.)

1 Samyutta-nikaya I p.62 has a reference to a disciple of the Buddha who travelled at a great speed to reach the end of the 'world.' The Buddha called him back saying that one can never reach the end of the 'world' by travelling (*gamanena na pattabbo lokassanto kudacanam*).

2 Instances such as 'the world is incomplete, insatiate, slave to desire" (*uno loko atitto tanhadaso... Ratthapala-sutta, Majjhima-nikaya* 82) and "I do not quarrel with the world; but the world quarrels with me" (*naham bhikkhave lokena vivadami, loko ca kho bhokkhave maya vivadati...*) *Samyutta-nikaya* III p.138.

3 Samyutta-nikaya I p.62: It is in this fathom-high carcass endowed with perception and mind that I make known the world, the origin of the world, the cessation of the world, and the way leading to the cessation of the world (*Bhikkhu Bodhi* (2000) p.158.)

4 *Samyutta-nikaya* V pp.420-424.

5 Bhikkhus, this life span of human beings is short. ... One who lives long, bhikkhus, lives a hundred years or a little longer.
Short is the life span of human beings—The good man should disdain it.
Connected Discourses of the Buddha, (Bhikkhu Bodhi 2000) p. 201.

6 Ibid.

7 Bhikhu Bodhi (2000) p. 551. (Samyutta-nikaya, Nidana Samyutta, II p. 25).

8 *Sumangalavilasini* (Commentary to the Dighanikaya) I p.432.

9 *Digha-nikaya* 27.

10 *Samyutta-nikaya* I p.62.

11 Consequently, the writers on the Buddhist view or attitude to nature describe Buddhism as holding a very admirable view of nature. An early example is: *Dharma Gaia: A Harvest of Essays in Buddhism and Ecology* (ed. Allan Hunt Berdiner, Parallax Press, Berkeley, California, 1990).

12 Ken Jones (1993 *Beyond Optimism: A Buddhist Political Ecology*, Oxford) seems to subscribe to a similar view when he complains that even the deeper ecological views are based on subtle forms of individualism. He advocates return to community. But since the community is the community of human beings, I do not think that we can overcome the issue of self-interest of human beings.

13 Refer to Malalasekera and Jayatilleke (1958) for an eloquent discussion on the Buddhist arguments for the oneness human race.

14 Vasettha sutta, *Majjhima-nikaya* 98.

15 Bhikkhu Bodhi (1995/2001) p. 801.

16 *Patimokkha* (being the collection of the monastic Vinaya rules).

17 Mano pubbangama dhamma—manosettha manomaya
Manasa ce padutthena—bhasati va karoti va
Tato nam dukkhamanveti—cakkamva vahato padam
...
Manasa ce pasannena—bhasati va karoti va
Tato nam sukhamanveti—chayava anapayini (*Dhammapada* 1-2)

18 *Sumanagalavilasini* (Commentary to the Dighanikaya) I p. 432.

19 *Digha-nikaya* 31.

20 Given its naturalistic understanding of human action (karma) and absence of a concept of creator God Buddhism does not consider disability to be a challenge to be accounted for.

21 *Samyutta-nikaya* V p. 2.

22 *Sutta-nipata* (Uraga-vagga) 8.

23 *Majjhima-nikaya* I p. 341.

24 *Dhammapada* 129.

25 *Anguttara-nikaya* I p.201.

26 Technically speaking, there is no (any other) punishment for parajika offences in the Vinaya for upon committing the offence one loses one's membership of the Sangha automatically, and the jurisdiction of the Vinaya does not extend to non-members. This

shows that the Buddhist punishment is primarily reformative.

27 *Anguttara-nikaya* II p.72.

28 *Dhammapada* 130.

29 *Samyutta-nikaya* II pp.189-190.

30 A view resembling this has been attributed to Pythagoras (Russell 1946 p. 59).

31 The problem of indirect responsibility for the death of the animal does not seem to have been raised or answered in the Pali discourses. The Mahayana tradition which observes strict vegetarianism is a notable exception to this T*heravada* standpoint.

32 'The Theravada Standpoint on Meat Eating", *Bul Gyo Hak Bo: Journal of Korean Buddhist Research Institute* No.50 (2008) pp. 77-96.

33 *Yassa rukkhassa chayaya—nisideyya sayeyya va*
Na tassa sakham bhindeyya—mittadubbhi hi papako: Bhuridatta-jataka 452.

34 *Vinaya* II pp. 207-235 (Vatta-khandhaka, Section on duties).

35 Translation from *Narada Thera* (1963/1993) p.94.

36 Vineyya loke abhijjha domanassam: *Digha-nikaya* II p.290.

37 Alagaddupama-sutta, *Majjhima-nikaya* 22.

Other References

Bhikkhu Bodhi, *The Connected Discourses of the Buddha,* Boston, Wisdom Publications, 2000.

Malalasekera, G.P. and Jayatilleke, K.N. *Buddhism and Race Question,* in the series on *The Race Question and Modern Thought,* Paris, UNESCO, 1958

Narada Thera, *The Dhammapada,* Taiwan: The Corporate Body of the Buddha Foundation, 1963/1993

Russell, Bertrand, *History of Western Philosophy,* London: George Allen and Unwin Ltd. 1946

6

Rajalakshmi

I am delighted to be present at this august meet and to share my thoughts on the subject of environmental consciousness, which has been profoundly pitted in the concept paper of this august meet against environmental regulations on which much emphasis has been made in recent times.

Environmental regulation is the institutional restraint on human propensity to invade and consume the environment and ecological resources beyond the capacity of nature to replace them. Based on science and logic, environmental regulation rests on external enforcement, particularly nation states, global treaties and courts.

But environmental consciousness is a voluntary restraint towards nature inherited by philosophies, faiths, and cultures and actualised through rituals, which prevent human deviance towards environment, and all living beings.

There is a paradigm difference between ecocentric philosophies, which see nature and humans as interrelated and integrated and anthropocentric ones that posit humans as the master and nature as subordinate. The world has been witnessing the rise, spread and domination of anthropocentric philosophies, faiths and ideologies through colonialism, modernity and globalisation.

While environmental consciousness tends and works to build an ecocentric society that consciously protects nature, environmental regulations work to contain an anthropocentric society which consciously erodes nature.

I will focus on environmental consciousness which is one of the fundamental themes of this meet.

Environmental consciousness is ingrained by tradition and rituals practised by communities, and sanctioned by religion, to live in harmony with nature maintaining the balance between nature and humans, and restraining them from making demands on nature beyond its capacity to replenish.

Deep environmental consciousness has been integral to human life in ancient times and are inherent in all ancient faiths and cultures all over the world.

The Hindu-Buddhist faiths and cultures, in particular, are ecocentric in their philosophy and practices by inseparably relating the humans and environment through faith and rituals. In Hinduism in particular, an elaborate ritualistic model exists which deeply ingrains environmental consciousness in humans.

I will limit my presentation to the aspect of environmental consciousness. In Hindu, Buddhist, Jain and Sikh philosophies the human is integral to environment and ecology and not apart from it or independent of it.

The four great spiritual streams, which emerged out of ancient India—Hinduism, Buddhism, Jainism and Sikhism, speak in one voice on how the entire universe—which includes humans—is one and inseparable entity.

The Hindu spiritual text Isavasya Upanisad, as translated by Mahatma Gandhi says, that everything down to the finest atom—the *panchabhutas*, earth, water, fire, air and space—is a manifestation of the divine.

The *Kalacharka Tantra*, the Buddhist scripture says Earth, water, air, fire and humans all emerged only out of the vacuum of space [*sunya*].

The Jain text Bhagwan Mahavira's Achara Sutra tells that *Panchabhutas*—earth, water, air, fire and space are not lifeless matter. They have *atma*—a soul

The Sikh text Guru Granth Sahib says the *Panchabhutas*—earth water air fire and space and all living beings.

They are strikingly similar not only in thought but also in words. The creation, the universe and the world are sacred, manifestation of the Divine, and not just secular or economic assets.

The humans are integral to the entire creation and not its master. That is how these four faiths propounded and expounded ecocentric human life as distinct from the current anthropocentric paradigm.

The consciousness that man is part of nature and not independent, and certainly not its master is fundamental to protect and sustain environment and ecology.

To ingrain, sustain and keep alive this consciousness and to internalise the idea of non-violence as much towards nature as towards fellow humans, the ecocentric faiths these faiths have built in a human life style which reveres nature.

The reverence for nature—seeing nature as manifestation of God or Divine or the Ultimate Reality—is inherent in these faiths and cultures.

The idea of reverence is not theoretical to be just spoken or written. It is to be practised and internalised through *samskarams* [a training module] practised in day to day life.

The Hindu philosophy has internalised the *samskarams* through symbols which exemplify and expound the themes of environment and ecology.

The Hindu culture has made tree a symbol of forests and prescribed *vriksha vandana*—reverence of tree—as the attitude of humans to forests. Unless humans revere the tree the forests are not safe.

The Hindu culture seeks to worship even wild animals, like snakes, as without wild animals the forests are left unprotected.

The science today has established a direct and mutual correlation between forest coverage and wild animal population—the decrease in one brings about the reduction in the other.

Likewise, Hindu culture prescribes worship of water—*Ganga vandana*—and earth—*Bhumi vandana*—and celebrates all rivers, lakes and ponds to inculcate environmental consciousness and protect water resources.

In the same way the Hindu culture inspires the faithful to worship the cow—*Gau Vandana*—worship the elephant—*Gaja Vandana*—and plants—*Tulsi vandana*—to inculcate ecological consciousness and ecological culture in humans.

So there are two aspects to environmental and ecological protection implicit in the Hindu philosophy:

> One, the thought and consciousness that man and nature are not independent but inseparable and integrated. This is fundamental to environmental and ecological protection. Here in philosophic terms humans see themselves as none superior to trees, plants, animals, water or a piece of earth. This includes even perceiving wild animals as the balancing phenomenon for environmental protection.
>
> Second, to actualise this consciousness the Hindu philosophy has prescribed

> *samskarams* [which are equated to rituals, which they are not] of reverence to trees, plants, and animals. The *samsarams* are voluntary subordination of man to concede to the superiority of nature of which the human himself is part.

These two aspects have sustained environment in India more than any law or regulation. Traditions are the most effective institutionalisation of environmental and ecological consciousness.

The Samvad series ought to continue to emphasise the environmental consciousness which are people centric and spiritual and promote ecocentric life on earth.

Environmental regulations, as the Prime Minister of India said in his speech, is an inferior protection to nature and environment as compared to aroused and deep environmental consciousness.

In the contemporary world, called modern world, environmental consciousness, which is spiritual in its origin and content, needs to be supported by education for maintaining, sustaining, explaining and rationalising deep environmental consciousness. The contemporary education needs to reviewed and restructured both in philosophy and content to internalise the spiritual values, *samskarams* and actualise environmental safeguards protection and celebration.

As a doctoral student in pursuit of further knowledge in economics at Sastra University in India, I appeal to the great religious and spiritual masters to commend to all nations to promote philosophies which inculcate environmental consciousness.

(Smt Rajalakshmi is Managing Trustee, Initiative for Moral and Cultural Training Foundation, Chennai, India)

7

Kathleen Thien

I am honoured to speak at the "Yangon Dialogue for Peace and Harmony – A Global Initiative for Conflict Avoidance and Environment Consciousness" on behalf of the Hindu Representative from Myanmar.

First of all, I would like to explain the greeting meaning of Namaste. We say Namaste to any religion, ethnicity, gender and age. This means, "I bow to the God who is keeping in your mind". In this way, the Hindus achieve peace, harmony and avoid conflict. As we all understand, the meaning of" peace "is "free from conflict". So that, peace does not only mean the end of conflict but it is a state of non-violence. "Ahimsa" is a fundamental principle of Hinduism that goes deeper than non-violence, prohibiting subtle abuse and even simple hurt. That's why "Ahimsa" is a good way to prevent the conflict. The idea of truth and non-violence is at the core of Mahatma Gandhi's political thought. Let me quote from Mahatma Gandhi's speech on peace. He said, "There is no way to peace, peace is the way". Thus, peace is very important for building solidarity and harmony. The world cannot survive without peace. If we do not have peace, conflict avoidance and environmental preservation will be impossible.

I have read that if we want peace, we must create peace in the hearts and minds of people. That's why, the role of religious leaders is very important in the "dialogue for peace, harmony and security "around the world. Religious leaders believe that all religions have the same goals, that of cultivating human goodness and bringing happiness to all human beings. If religious leaders contribute to an atmosphere of peace and harmony, it will have a positive impact on society.

As we all know, if we want to take the initiative for to avoid conflict and preserve the environment, we also need to know the peace building and managing conflicts basic skills No matter where we live, conflict can affect our community, our country and our world. People of any race, gender, social, status and age can be affected by conflicts. From morning till night, we hear about the conflict, war, violence and crime around the world. So that, our environment loses peace day by day. Of course, we all know that conflict avoidance is the best solution. As I mentioned, the basis for conflict avoidance is non-violence (Ahimsa). But, how? In my opinion, mutual understanding is vital for avoiding conflict. It is so crucial that we need to educate community members as much as possible. Moreover, the role of a mediator is often important for global conflict avoidance and environmental consciousness. Mediators need a lot of different skills and support from a professional team to get to the root causes and conflict dynamics. That's why, participation of a wide range of civil society actors in the mediation process is also important to reduce conflict.

Here, I would like to highlight the importance of the role of women in the mediation processes. Culturally, very few Asian women, especially (Hindu Women in Myanmar) participate in the public discussions on peace, harmony and security. But, in my view, women should be part of the formal negotiation on equal footing with men, and act as mediators, themselves. Women are able to bring new ideas to their families and communities. That's why, it is important that women are enabled to nurture a culture of peace both in the home and the community.

Moreover, children should be taught about peace at home from a young age. This will teach families to be peaceful within their home, to settle arguments. So that, children will come to realise the role of religion in conflict resolution and peace building when they grow up.

According to Mahatma Gandhi, "If we want to reach real peace in this world, we should start educating children". Swami Vivekananda also said:

> We have all been hearing from childhood of such things as love, peace, charity, equality, and universal brotherhood; but they become to us mere words without meaning, words which we repeat like parrots, and it has become quite natural for us to do so. For this reason, children should be taught the real meaning of peace, harmony and security instead of repeating like parrots.

Thus we need to work together for peace between generations and to give young people throughout the world real hope for future.

I would like end with a quote from the speech of former Secretary General of the United Nations Mr. Kofi Annan. In his speech he said, "We may have different religions, different languages, different coloured skin, but we all belong to be one human race."

That's why I would like to say that a dialogue for peace, harmony and security is a bridge for our human race. Without this bridge, we will never get peace in this world.

I conclude with the Peace (*Shanthi*) prayer.

Om, Sarve bhavanu sukhinah,
Sarve shantu niramayah,
Sarve bhadarani pashyntu
Ma kashid - dukkha bhaal bhave

Om, May all become happy.
May all become free from illness?
May all see what is auspicious,
Let no one suffer.
Om, peace, peace, peace!

[Kathleen Thein (Kalpana Kumari) is Chairperson of Hindu Women of Faith Net Association & Executive Committee Member of Peaceful Myanmar Initiative]

8

Bhikkhuni Dhammananda

IN my previous involvement on a research on Buddhism and Nature Conservation in 1985, we had discovered that the message on Environmental concern is expressed very strongly in Buddhism as compared to other world religions, i.e. Christianity or Islam. It has been more than three decades since and academics are more and more interested in the message delivered by the Buddha, more than 2500 years ago, yet very pertinent to the problems the world faces today.

This paper will touch on the philosophical exposition provided in Buddhist texts and its applicability to crisis as we humans are now facing.

How Buddhism Views the World?

The world is not created by God as the theists would believe. According to Buddhism all natural phenomena are accounted for in terms of the Law of Dependent Originations. (*Paticcasamuppada*) viz:

1. What this is, that is (= when A is, B is)
2. This arising, that arising (= A arising, B arising)
3. When this is not, That is not (= When A is not, B is not)
4. This ceases, that ceases (A ceases, B ceases)

This is how we look at things around us. This interdependent characteristic applies to everything including Nature itself. We see nature as one unique whole, whatever happens causes ripples and affects other existing things and beings around it.

When a tree falls, it affects several other living things that depend on the existence of the particular tree. That is to say when one is moved everything else moves.

It is a grave mistake when a government officer looks at the tree and sees its value in cubic meters of wood only. In reality that one tree is related and inter-related with all things around it. Thus, one tree is linked to the whole eco-system in that particular forest.

Buddhist Theory of Creation

How Do Buddhists Look at Theory of Creation?

In Jewish and Christian tradition we are familiar with how the world was created by God, and how man came into the world. Then a woman was created out of a man (rib story). But in Buddhism, we have another story.

Reading through *Aggannasutra*, previously human beings were divine, shining objects, but with desire, they came down to consume and took a liking in the worldly substance. Thus they lost their luminosity and took the form of man and woman. Man and woman came into being in the same manner.

Interesting part mentioned in the same sutra is that natural degradation is brought about by the decline in moral standard of the king and the ministers. For the first time, we have a glimpse of the cause and effect relationship between human activities and the balance of nature.

In the words of the Buddha, this is how we read in *Aggannasutra*:

> *At such time, monks, as rajahs (kings) are unrighteous, the ministers of rajahs also are unrighteous. When ministers are unrighteous, Brahmins and householders are also unrighteous, thus, townsfolk and villagers are unrighteous. This being so, moon and sun go wrong in their courses. This being, constellations and stars do likewise; days and nights, months and fortnights, seasons and years are out of joint; the winds blow wrong, out of season. Thus the Devas (gods) are annoyed. This being so, they sky-god bestows not sufficient rain. Rains not falling seasonably, the crops ripen in wrong season, men who lived on such crops are short-lived, ill-favoured, weak and sickly.*

On the contrary when kings are righteous so are the ministers and the rest, nature goes about in its normal course, thus the Buddha concluded:

> *When carts are crossing, if the bull goes straight,*
> *They all go straight because his course is straight.*

So among men, if he who's reckoned best
Lives righteously, the others do so too.
The whole realm dwells in happiness if the rajah lives aright.
(Anguttara Nikaya, vol. III PTS, 1960, E. Hare tr.)

It is quite clear, from Buddhist point of view things are interdependent and thus conditional upon each other as the laws of Buddhist dialectic prevail, where by when A is, B is, and so on, as we have seen above. It is clear that by cause and effect, the sequences of events play a significant role in nature. This is quite important and practical because it means we can direct the situation at hand and work out what is desirable by creating a favourable cause and condition. More important than rectifying the world outside, is the need to understand that the physical world is affected directly from the inner world. When a person is well trained spiritually, it affects the physical world in a positive manner. Thus we see how eco-ethics is the keyword that we cannot overlook easily.

Buddhist Attitudes Towards Environment

All the important events in Buddha's life took place in natural setting. Buddhist monks in the early period lived in natural surroundings. It is not a surprise to find many of monastic rules set by the Buddha clearly set a message for respect of natural environment.

The monks lived in the forest, thus had to pay respect to their environment, they're not only forbidden to harm trees, but also mandated to protect it. The monks were to use natural resources only for their needs and not to exploit them. This was clear in the instruction how monks can break only the amount of tooth wood needed, rather than break the whole branch, and throw away the rest.

As for the preservation of water, it was also clearly instructed in a *jataka* story how the birds who caused the droppings in the water thus polluted the water were punished by the angry *naga*.

Humans are seen as part of nature, thus harming nature eventually brings about destruction of mankind.

In this fast moving materialistic society, a temple can still be a seat of learning. Monks and nuns can bring about the teaching of the Buddha and lead society with respect to nature. Re-use and recycle has been expressed even as early as the Buddha's time. When Ven. Ananda explained how he was going to use the 500 offered robes to the *sangha*. He explained the use and re-use of the robe in a very practical manner. He hence convinced the King to offer another 500 robes to the *sangha*.

When we talk about environment, we should not focus only trees and water resources. Human beings are also part of our environment.

How are we responsible to all human beings in order to keep our environment healthy?

All the material world around us is the product of human mind, it is therefore of utmost important that we need to create material environment to match our spiritual environment, in a friendly manner.

Buddhism is one religion that has a clear awareness of this importance. At every session of meditation, there is always a spread of loving kindness accrued from training of the mind. When the mind is well trained, the sharing of loving kindness at the end of session is very effective. It causes a positive vibration around us, with unconditional sharing of this loving kindness. Buddhism is therefore, very advanced in its message for the protection of the environment.

Buddhist Practice

The Buddha established the fourfold Buddhist communities during the very early period of his mission. This happened when he was newly enlightened and the Mara came to remind him that he should now pass away as he already achieved enlightenment. The Buddha did not accept his invitation until he had established the fourfold Buddhist communities, i.e. *Bhikkhu, Bhikkhuni, Upasaka* and *Upasika*. He also expected them to study his teaching, put it into practice and also be able to defend his teaching.

We noted that Buddhism is not about textual study only but emphasizes also on the practice. Unless the teaching are put into practice, his disciples cannot speak from direct experience. Buddhism is be lived, not to be only learnt.

Once when we live our life as true Buddhists then we understand the interconnectedness of things in nature, and realize the interdependent nature of things. Buddhists will be great care takers of nature and its environment.

The Buddhist message on Nature and environment holds equally true now as it was then. The mega problems that the world faces now is simply because we do not take heed of the message that the Buddha guided us some 2600 years ago. It is not too late that we, humankind, be humble and approach Nature in a proper manner.

(Dr. Chatsumarn Kabilsingh, ordained Dhammananda Bhikkhuni, is a Theravādin bhikkuṇi (Buddhist nun) and serves as the absess of the only temple in Thailand)

ROUND TABLE OF THE SPIRITUAL MASTERS

1

Thich Duc Thien

IT is a fact that conflicts do occur in the process of social development and evolution. Conflicts could be within oneself, one's family, between ethnics, nations or territories. Conflicts lead to wars, death and sufferings for mankind. Therefore, people have always been looking for solutions everywhere, and in religions to avoid conflicts.

In this paper, I emphasize on what the Lord Buddha taught in His teaching, which first appeared in India more than 2600 years ago, still hold true today, and can provide perfect solutions to address global problems, and build a truly harmonious and peaceful community and society.

According to Lord Buddha, the true solution to ending conflicts needs to focus on ending the causes for the disputes. Buddhism believes that solutions are just temporary and does not appreciate those temporary solutions, because if the deep causes of conflicts and wars are not eliminated permanently at the root level, solutions will only work temporarily, wars and conflicts will happen again and again, and will continue when there are new causes for a dispute. Therefore, if one can recognize the cause for a dispute and conflict internally or externally, he can prevent conflicts from happening.

In both, the Theravada scriptures in the *Pali* Canon and the Mahayana sutras in Sanskrit manuscripts present the same teachings of Lord Buddha which identify the root causes, both internal and external, for a dispute. In order to reach conflict avoidance, one must recognize the cause for dispute and conflict as written in the *Sāmagāma Sutra*:

> "*Ananda*, there are six causes for a dispute. What are the six causes? When the *Bhikkhu* becomes angry and bears a grudge, he becomes unruly even

> towards the Teacher, rebels against the Teaching and becomes unruly, rebels against the community and becomes unruly, does not live complete in the training. Thus he arouses a dispute in the community, for the unpleasantness of many and the unpleasantness of gods and men. *Ananda*, if you see this cause for a dispute internally or externally, you should make effort for the dispelling of that cause for a dispute, and for its non-arising again…Again, *Ananda*, the *Bhikkhu* is merciless with hypocrisy... jealous and selfish... crafty and fraudulent..., is with evil desires and wrong view... holding fast to worldly matters and not giving up easily. When the *Bhikkhu* holds fast to worldly matters and does not give up easily, he becomes unruly even towards the Teacher, rebels against the teaching and becomes unruly, rebels against the Community and becomes unruly, does not live complete in the training. Thus, he arouses a dispute in the community, for the unpleasantness of many and the unpleasantness of gods and men…*Ananda*, if you see this cause for a dispute internally or externally, you should make effort for the dispelling of that cause for a dispute, and for its non-arising again. This is dispelling the evil causes of disputes, for their non-arising in the future. *Ananda*, these are the six causes for disputes."[1]

We can generalize the causes for a dispute in the world today from the following specific causes:

> First: greed, hatred, ignorance. The three poisons mentioned in the sutras.
> Second: *Avidyā* or ignorance and the lack of knowledge.
> Third: economics and materialism.
> Fourth: poverty.
> Fifth: fanaticism.
> Sixth: intolerance towards different ideologies and political viewpoints.

The three poisons are the causes of human sufferings. Greed essentially means desire and extreme attachment. Greed can never be satisfied, and it is the companion of hatred, envy, and dispute, which lead to conflicts when desires are not satisfied. Hatred brings unhappy feelings, which fuels anger and detestation. Anger and hatred come from greed and lust and *avidyā*. *Avidyā* leads to poverty, fanaticism and intolerance towards different ideologies and political viewpoints, which causes conflicts and wars.

Buddhist principles point out that the three poisons within each human being are related to the social conditions in which he lives. If everyone is aware of the three poisons as well as the causes and methods for overcoming them, we will have great results through the practice of *kusala karma* and benevolence. Those poisons can be transformed into benevolent energy, violence and conflicts will be transformed into love and peace, and true happiness will rise. Buddhists believe that inner unity and harmony would lead to outer unity and harmony. When living and working together in harmony, it leads to integral harmony. When the major causes of conflict among individuals and societies are recognized correctively as greed, hatred and ignorance, the removal of these psychological hindrances would bring unity, harmony, peace and happiness in the community.

In the *Sangha* Community, to prevent and settle potential and existing conflicts, Lord Buddha taught that each *Bhikkhu* must live harmoniously, training on the six rules of *kusala karma* with their body, speech and mind. These rules can be applied to our society today, namely:

(1) Our bodily actions should be towards others with love and compassion.
(2) Our verbal actions should be towards others with love and compassion.
(3) Our mental actions should be towards others with love and compassion.
(4) Food should be shared equally.
(5) Moral disciplines should be equal.
(6) Experience should be shared in releasing sufferings and gaining true happiness.

As written in the *Samagama Sutra,* "*Ananda*, there are six things that promote unity, gladness and friendship, and dispel disputes. What are the six? *Ananda*, the *Bhikkhu* should be established in bodily actions of loving kindness towards co-associates in the holy life openly and secretly. The *Bhikkhu* should be established in verbal actions of loving kindness towards co-associates in the holy life openly and secretly. The *Bhikkhu* should be established in mental actions of loving kindness towards co-associates in the holy life openly and secretly. Again the *Bhikkhu* shares equally all rightful gains so far as the morsels put in the bowl, with the virtuous co-associates in the holy life. Again the *Bhikkhu* becomes equal in all virtues that are not spotted, fissured, free of blemish, and praised by the wise as conducive to concentration with the co-associates in the holy life. Again the *Bhikkhu* shares the noble view that rightfully destroys unpleasantness, of one who logically thinks about it, with the co-associates in the holy life openly and secretly. *Ananda*, these six things promote unity, gladness and friendship and dispel disputes. *Ananda*, do you see a single word which is not acceptable among these words? I do not see." Therefore *Ananda*, be accomplished in these six things that promote unity, gladness and friendship and dispels disputes, it will be for your welfare for a long time."[2]

Lord Buddha has taught us the principles for preventing wars and conflicts, namely integrity, mutual respect, regular dialogues, acceptance of differences, sharing of interests, spreading benevolence, practicing resignation and accommodation, which are necessary principles to be practiced for the avoidance of conflicts. According to Lord Buddha, religious and political leaders have a crucial role in preventing conflicts and wars. A good and responsible leader will lead his country in peace and guide everyone towards the good path. Political leaders should take appropriate measures to strengthen universal peace by respecting the territorial integrity or political independence of all nations. Political leaders, governments should be promoted in solving international issues based on respect for international laws. Religious leaders should encourage their followers to respect cultural heritage and diversity, to practice religious tolerance in building and promoting religious harmony and world peace. Religious leaders should encourage constructive interaction and dialogue among cultures, civilizations and religions. Interfaith dialogue provides crucial contributions to confidence building and harmonious building among religions. Through interfaith dialogue, we can search for and gain a better understanding of common ethical values of all faiths which help us address and resolve common challenges threatening human society, including climate change, environmental crisis, social crisis, conflicts and terrorism.

Today, the teachings of Lord Shakyamuni Buddha are truly effective solutions to addressing the above global problems because Buddhism's methodology is to address the problems from their root causes, preventing them from happening rather than remedying and looking for solutions after they already happen. Like Indian Prime Minister Narendra Modi said at the Samvad Forum in New Delhi in 2015[3] that: the international society mechanism is showing more and more limitations in addressing countless disputes of the world. Therefore, it is no surprise that the world is taking note of Buddhism ideology and expects that this ideology will be the miraculous key in the determination to eliminate conflicts.

(Most Venerable Dr. Thich Duc Thien is the Secretary General, National Vietnam Buddhist Sangha and Vice Rector, Vietnam Buddhist University in Hanoi)

REFERENCES

1 Sàmagàma Sutra, Translated from Pali by Bhikkhu Bodhi

2 Ibid.

3 www.vifindia.org/Vivekananda International Foundation/New Delhi-2015

2

Swami Govind Dev Giri

We are currently running 30 Vedic Schools and also serving Rev. Gurudev Swami Satyamitranand Giriji Maharaj through Bharatmata Mandir presided over by Swami Avadeshananda Giriji. I am delighted to find myself among great people here who are very seriously thinking for world peace, harmony and security. If we have to make progress in this way, we shall have to find the solution on many levels.

The first thing we should see is the philosophical level. Unless we find some solution on philosophical level, ethical level, social level and also on the religious level, we can't proceed to achieve our goal. Our friends have said that first of all the mind must be cultured. If the mind, which is the breeding ground of violence, is to be pacified, we will have to cultivate the five *yamas* following Patanjali—namely Ahimsa, *Satya, Asteya, Brahmacharya and Asangraha*. The same has been advocated by Bhagawan Tathagata Buddha as *Panchasheela*. The ways of Patanjali, Bhagawan Buddha and the Bhagavadgita are in fact one and the same. Therefore, on the ethical level we will have to encourage people to tread the path of truthfulness, non-violence, non-greediness and other virtues.

We will have to preach this, but we will also have to have a philosophical basis for what we preach. This has been given by Bhagawan Adi Shankaracharya. In fact, it is originally given by the Vedas and it has been explained in detail by Bhagawan Adi Shankaracharya as the philosophy of *Advaita* (Non-dualism). According to it, ultimately there is no duality. The whole reality, animate or inanimate, is one. This has also been scientifically established by the famous scientist Fritzoff Kapra in his book 'The Tao of Physics'. According to him, if physics has to make any progress, it shall have to step into the metaphysics of India, the philosophy of non-dualism. If we are essentially one, and many only superficially, then anything done against anybody else is ultimately done against myself only. I am reminded of a quote from Shrimad Bhagavatam, one up on the '*Ishavasyamidam Sarvam*', that says '*Atmavasyamidam Vishwam*', 'the whole world is but my extension; the observer and the observed are one.' Hence, if the world is but my extension, then anything done to harm anybody else, is ultimately against myself.

A person with the right vision sees everybody in himself and himself in everybody. As such, going against anybody is going against oneself. Therefore, this philosophical doctrine must be preached and accepted by all. It is no doubt true that this sense of affinity or brotherhood is observed in many instances, but it is limited to the people of one's own faith, not to those of other faiths. This is also supported by some scriptures and hence is taken seriously, leading to a divisive attitude. In these circumstances, we need to follow the formula of Vedavyas in his *Brahmasutras*—'*Tat tu Samanvayat*'—meaning we will have to interpret such scriptural commands in a reconciliatory, inclusive way so that it leads to peace and harmony. In India, this has been done for ages. But for this, our reason should be used in a constructive and not in a destructive way. Each one of us in this august assembly commands a position of respect and authority in the society. Our followers follow our words unquestioningly. So, the responsibility of guiding them in a constructive way lies on the shoulders of each one of us here.

Similarly, we will also have to work on the social level as well. I hail from a rural background and have experienced myself that people belonging to all faiths—Hindus, Muslims, Christians, Jains or Buddhist—used to intermingle harmoniously. But in the last couple of decades, the atmosphere has changed. Discord has been deliberately created. Hence, we will have to be cautious.

In this connection, I would like to narrate my latest experience. Last week, the CM of MP, Mr. Shivaraj Singh Chauhan invited me for a meeting of his newly created Anand Foundation and asked for my views. I told him that the various means he is devising to ensure happiness of people may be effective for a while, but not in the long run. Ultimately, people can find happiness only in Spirituality. I suggested that we should have an *Anand Katha* where people can see preachers and saints of all faiths share the same dais speaking the same language. As sage Narada says in his Bhaktisutras—true happiness and peace lie only in devotion of the Almighty. Whatever our differences, we all agree on devotion to the Almighty. You will notice that there are diverse scriptures and that they are interpreted by scholars differently. But the saints belonging to these faiths have *'lived'* these scriptures and hence have spoken the same language of love. An assembly of the followers of such Saints is bound to create harmony, peace and security.

(Swami Govind Dev Giri ji is founder of Maharshi Ved Vyas Prathisthan, India)

3

Arayawangso

HUMAN, society, and religion (*dhamma*) are components that have long been supportive of and relying on each other, for the integrated development of *Dhamma*. Therefore, the true role and duty of human beings must be to conduct themselves with *Dhamma*, to have respect for *Dhamma*, and to practice *Dhamma* properly.

All human society must have religion, theory, and belief embedded in their spirits which have continued to be passed on in the form of culture, custom and tradition, reflecting the nature of that particular religion, theory or belief.

In fact, all religions come under the same general law of *Dhamma* but the level of *Dhamma* each of them is classified depends on the spiritual quality of the people which must be significantly influenced by the environment in that part of the world. So we see a wide variety of teachings which do not pose a conflict if we consider the objective, that is, requiring humanity to attain benefit and happiness with *Dhamma*, under the context of the same *Dhamma*.

Therefore, different teachings of each religion is not an issue for debate which could only lead to discordance and destruction among the followers. It is important to know how to find benefit and virtue in the teaching of each religion in order to integrate them at the fundamental level, enabling them to relate to each other, to join in the elimination of conflict or avoid the division which will arise in human society.

It is a worthwhile effort to properly utilize the basic good quality of each religion at the right time and right occasion. And if we can weave the spirits of humanity together with the teaching of each religion so they can coexist harmoniously, despite the difference among nations, religions, caste, sex and age. That should be truly correct and it is believed that humanity has such aspiration.

The world is currently heated up with harmful actions, rivalries and greediness, illogical and immoral attacks by planting thoughts and beliefs that are antagonistic to the teachings of all religions. It is the major duty of humanity to bring religion back into the life systems, to use the power of *Dhamma* derived from the study and practice according to *Dhamma* teaching, to entirely eliminate problems that would lead to the destruction and encroachment among humanity, as happened in the past.

Buddhism was born in Jambudvipa 45 years before the Buddhist Era. The Exulted One who established Buddhism was the former "Prince Siddhattha" of Sakhaya royal lineage, with the clan name of Gotama, in the Khattiya Caste of Kabilavastu City, Sakhaya State. He attained supreme enlightenment by Himself under the Great Bodhi Tree, on the bank of Nerunjara River, Uruvela, Magadha State.

Dhamma principle that He was self-enlightened is called *ariyasacca* 4, meaning the Four Noble Truths: *Dukkha, Samudaya, Nirodha,* and *Magga. Magga ariyasacca* is the Noble Path of practice for the realization of the Noble Truth, for the extinction of sufferings *(nibbana)*.

> This demonstrates the specific characteristic of Buddhism that it is pragmatic—can be tested by practice, trained and proved by oneself, based on *sila, samadhi,* and *panna* (morality, concentration, and wisdom), known as *Tisikkha* (the threefold trainings) or the practice of the Holy Life (*brahmacariya*) which can develop life towards independence and liberation by mind cultivation according to Buddhist teachings.

Although the ultimate aim of Buddhism is to develop life towards liberation, not being enslaved to the world, it lays down the basic teachings in a number of aspects, to develop a person to have virtue and ethics and to be truly worthy, leading to the management and supervision of the worldly domain (society) to have peace with happiness, with the system consisting of *Dhamma*, which is the virtue system for the building of global peace.

This is evidenced in His exhortation to bhikkhus to go forth for the welfare and support of the many, out of compassion for the world, for the benefit and happiness of God and human, teaching *Dhamma* that is beautiful in the beginning (*sila*), in the middle (*samadhi*), and in the ending (*panna*). It is the proclamation of the holy life in study and practice that is complete with meanings and letters that are perfectly purified.

Buddhism lays down the principles that lead towards the transformation of life's value by elevating the spiritual cultivation with the power of *Dhamma* arising from the study and practice. Managing education for the development of life, to progress towards human's full potential, by having knowledge that is coupled with virtue, is therefore the key identity of Buddhism, with the confidence that peace can only occur when humanity are able to develop life to attain the status of noble being, with the power of mindful wisdom that can be self-generated.

Developing a person to have mindful wisdom is the heart of managing study and practice of Buddhism, with the aspiration to create the virtue system—in economics, politics, and governance, to lead the nation's society and global community towards peace and happiness with *Dhamma*. Doing so requires that human have morality, ethics and virtue by the cultivation of mindful wisdom in the conduct of life for the elevation of life to be independent and liberated from the power of worldly conditions.

To produce human resources that is rational, know how to use their wisdom for careful deliberation, not be deluded and gullible, have the right view in accordance with natural truth, to penetrate various phenomena with wisdom, knowing right from wrong by themselves, capable of thinking independently, to learn how to think properly, and use the thought rightly in accordance with *Dhamma* (*sammaditthi*).

This is the main task in Buddhism: to bring back to society the good, knowledgeable and virtuous persons, so they can use their knowledge, virtue and goodness for the design of society that is good and proper according to *Dhamma* benefit, enabling peace to emerge in that society.

Buddhism is both a religion and an academic science, for the creation of benefit and happiness for all humanity. It is thus a religion that is humanistic, and altruistic, with love for fellow human beings, faith in human's intellectual wisdom to build peace and happiness for individual, society and nation.

Therefore Buddhism does not aim merely at the development of an individual, but has laid down the principle of lending support to the environment under the context of democratic society, as evidenced in the governing principle that is beneficial and supportive of the worldly domain (nation's society), from the level of individual, to that of family, community, society, nation, and global community, with the belief that the world and *Dhamma* must rely on each other, albeit with different role, duty, and responsibility.

The teaching that aims towards the building of peace and happiness for an individual, society, nation and all humanity is the heart of Buddhism which lays down its teachings with regard to *Dhamma* as being supreme, displaying respect for the Rule of Righteousness as the core principle in the administration and management of general society. Its purpose is to create all levels of people to have knowledge that is proper with *Dhamma*, to conduct their lives with *Dhamma* and to be virtuous.

Most importantly, they must be capable of creating *Dhamma* in that nation's society, to bring about justice for all, leading to society that can realize true peace with happiness. All these must depend on the power of *Dhamma* emanating from the study of and practice according to *Dhamma* teachings that the Blessed One had well expounded, for the benefit of all beings, for them to conduct themselves with *Dhamma*, to be reverence of *Dhamma*, and to practice *Dhamma* properly, which will then bring about the return of *Dhamma* power that will protect *Dhamma* practitioners, so that they will encounter only true benefit and happiness with *Dhamma*.

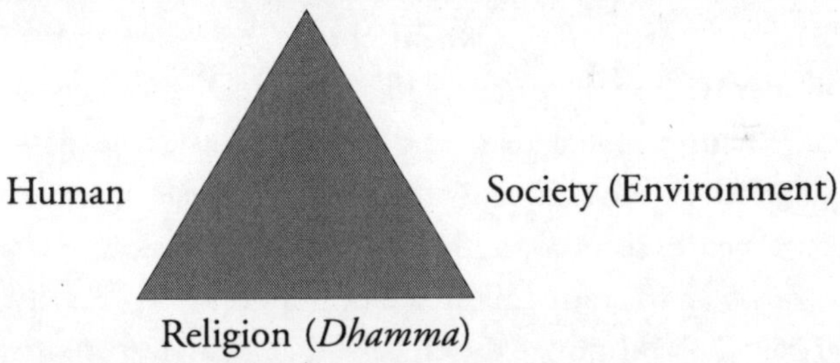

Humanity's Life Development System

A Balanced Relations between Human, Society (Environment) and Religion (*Dhamma*).

(Venerable Arayawangso is Abbot, Buddhapojhariphunchai Forest Monastery Lamphun, Thailand)
(English translation by Dr. Pawadee Tonguai)

4

U Aung Thein Nyunt

As we all know, societies, states and individuals around the world today, have brimming advantages of unparalled advancement in technology and modes of communication. At the same time due to the uneven standard of living and diverse propensities for violence and conflict based on different religious faith, there is no safety in daily life as well as there are the issues of disparity, vulnerability and threat to daily life created by natural disasters and human beings by themselves.

In most parts of the world there also arise political and economic instabilities with social unrest, chaos, violence, conflicts and fighting. At this critical juncture global religious leaders, political leaders and social leaders together with all their citizens and philanthropists have to give utmost priority to ensure peace, security, and the good life. No country in the world is in a balmy position to enjoy fullest extent of peace and security that they long for. Moreover, the additional problem all are facing currently, is the menace of religious extremists who have no knowledge of the intrinsically profound inner-core of their own religion.

In every religion of the world there are indeed many ethical and law-abiding instructions and ways of living which can make their followers calm down and contented in removing anger, hatred and animosity. To the best of our knowledge every religion should be a powerful and sturdy implement to make its believers enjoy peace, harmony and security.

Here are some noteworthy excerpts from the sacred texts of different religious faiths:

- What is hateful to you, do not do to your fellow human being. (Judaism, Talmud, Shabbat, 31);
- Do nothing unto others which would cause you pain if it were done to you. (Hinduism, Mahabharata, 5:1517);
- We should regard all creatures as we regard our own self. (Jainism, Mahavir);
- Do for others what you want them to do for you. (Christianity, Matthew, 7:12);
- None of you is a believer untill he desires for his brother that which he desires for himself. (Islam, Sunnah);
- Do not create emity with anyone, for God is within everyone. (Sikhism, Guru Granth Sahib, 259); and
- What you do not want done to you do not do to others. (Confucianism, Analects, 15:23).

  (Ref: The Lion Encyclopedia: WORLD RELIGION, by David Self: printed in Thailand, 2010, p.123, with headline: "the Golden Rule".)

Despite such noble and virtuous instructions or ways of living embedded in the noble mind or intellectual goodwill of every religion, the world we live in is often driven by religious conflicts and sectarian strife or even war and brutal fighting. Paying deep attention only to the outer-appearance of the religion and neglecting its inner-core without substantial application of the genuine teachings, most of the religious followers make the world unbalanced and unstable. Thus there is no loving-kindness, no compassion, no sympathetic joy, no self understanding, no tolerance, no forgiveness in the realm of their minds, being full of dark thoughts.

We all have to explore and collaborate on how moderation and conflict avoidance can play a vital role in supporting, maintaining, and enhancing peace, harmony, security, stability and prosperity within the context of communities, governments as well as international institutions.

To build a global conflict avoidance architecture among multi-faith and multi-ethnic societies across the globe, it is crucially important to support one's own religion as it is to be approachable and agreeable to other beliefs in order to say what everyone can agree on.

The founders, prophets and teachers of all the major faiths have tried to show the way towards a better future. While their teachings remain distinctive and special to their followers they have enough in common for people to live in peace with another and to discover a meaning and purpose for their lives. It is very important for everyone to establish peace within, in compliance with the respective noble teachings of religions. We have to try our best by ourselves, without seeking any other outside help.

The Buddha taught:

- "One should first establish oneself in what is prosper; then only should one instruct others. Let not the wise man defile himself for reproach. (Dham: 158)"
- "Whoever seeks his own happiness by causing pain to others, is not released from hatred, being himself entangled in the tangles of hatred. (Dham: 291)"
- "In those who harbour such thoughts: "He abused me, struck me, overpowered me, robbed me", hatred is never appeased. (Dham: 3)"
- "In those who do not cherish such thoughts: "He abused me, struck me, overpowered me, robbed me", hatred is appeased. (Dham: 4)"
- "Conquest breeds enmity; the defeated lives in pain; happily the peaceful lives, giving up both victory and defeat. (Dham: 201)"

Today's youngsters will become elders in future; only good youngsters will become good elders; only the good elders can create good families; only the good families can create good streets, good villages, good towns, and cities—only the good citizens can build a global conflict avoidance architecture.

In this age of globalization, people of different races, cultures, and religions have come to live and work together much more closely than at any other times in history and multi-racial, multi-cultural societies have become a global phenomenon. Along with this emergence, also arose unwelcome aftereffects of biases and prejudices simultaneously creating hate-speech and hate-action, racial and religious conflicts, and worst of them extremism and terrorism.

Greed, craving, hatred or animosity among human beings are constructed on the basis of delusion and ignorance. Extremists of greed and craving are like the ones who insert inflammable materials into flames and extremists of hatred and animosity are similar to those who burn the burning world. Everybody, regardless of race and religion, commits these unwelcome and unwholesome actions according to the inherent nature of the worldlings-average people. To avoid both of these extremes and to tread on the moderate or middle path, all the religious leaders, political leaders or national leaders have the responsibility to work together in unity and to lead all global people onto this moderate or middle path.

Although every religion teaches their followers not to commit evils, to do good—verbally and bodily, and to establish purification of mind, most of the followers stay aloof from these teachings, neglecting to put them into actual practice. Besides, some religious teachers and instructors misinterpret the original genuine teachings and lead their followers onto the wrong way as they want to make use of them in the wrongful situation. Therefore, first and foremost, we all must pay attention to the collection of genuine religious teachings and virtuous and devout religionists.

For investigating the fundamentals of different religions by means of a constructive dialogue among religions we need good citizens to be replete with the knowledge of their respective genuine teachings and moral virtue. Only such virtuous and devout religionists can establish the conflict avoidance architecture and maintain peace and security among diverse religions.

We all have to make an arduous attempt for treading on 'the Moderate Path'—which means the observance of moral ethics, giving charity, following the principles, pure and platonic love, compassion and goodwill, patience and understanding, and the last—the practice of 'insight-meditation'. (which can be carried out by everyone, regardless of race and creed). After we have purified our mind or been blessed with intellectual goodwill, showing a good example to our followers we should organize our followers and lead to the path on which we have already successfully trodden and impart the intrinsic genuine teachings of our respective religion, without leaving the grassroot-level followers of ours.

To avoid religious conflict and to build peace, harmony and security, "intellectual goodwill within" plays the vital role. Without it, however many arduous attempts we all may make in different ways and means, we cannot achieve it. In order to construct a Conflict Avoidance Architecture for well-being of all diverse religious followers, let us initiate "Intellectual Goodwill Within, now."

(Mr. U Aung Thein Nyunt is Director General, Department of Religious Affairs, Govt of Myanmar)

5

Lokesh Muni

I represent Jain faith of religion and feel that Religion, Peace and Harmony are two sides of the same coin. Religious Harmony creates sense of security.

Religion has a definite role to play in people's search for world peace. We can create a sense of security among people by resolving conflicts and creating religious harmony. The moral principles and values contained in teachings of great religious teachers are essential factors for the reduction and ultimate eradication of greed, hatred, and delusion that form the root cause of various conflicts and wars. Within oneself, these three evil or unwholesome roots bring about great unrest in the mind, resulting in physical outbursts of violence culminating in global warfare.

The fact that war begins in the minds of people is well recognized by certain peace-loving people. The preamble to UNESCO's constitution says: "Since wars begin in the minds of men, it is in the minds of men that the defenses of peace must be constructed." That is, if one wishes to have peace of mind, one must also construct defenses of peace in one's own mind.

The world cannot have peace until nations and people begin to reduce their selfish desires for more and more material possessions, give up their racial arrogance, and eliminate their madness for worldly power. Material wealth alone cannot bring peace and happiness to the minds of people. The key to real and lasting peace lies in "mental disarmaments"—disarming the mind from all kinds of "poisonous" defilements such as greed, hatred, jealousy, egotism, etc.

Religion not only inspires and guides people but also provides them with the necessary tools to reduce greed with the practice of charity; to overcome hate and aversion with loving-kindness; and to remove ignorance with the development of wisdom and insight, in order to understand the true nature of beings and "see things as they really are."

The negative aspects of religion lie in the madness of some so-called religionists who try to convert and win followers by hook or by crook, rather than adhering to proper instruction and guidance. The purposeful misinterpretation of scriptural texts for various ulterior motives has led to religious persecutions, inquisitions, and "holy wars." These terribly awful experiences have really marred the very name "religion."

In context of today's spiritual needs, religionists should work together in earnestness and not in jealous competition with one another. They must work in harmony and cooperate in the true spirit of service for the welfare and happiness of the many. It is only then that they can effectively influence the opinions of the masses and truly educate the people with some higher values of life, which are very necessary for peaceful co-existence and integrated human development.

Differences in religious beliefs and practices should not hinder the progress of various religionists working for a common cause, for world peace. Let all religions teach people to be good and proclaim the brotherhood of humankind. Let religions teach people to be kind, to be tolerant and to be understanding.

Enough suffering and destruction have been caused by human "cleverness." It is time that we pause and reflect upon the true values of religion and seek proper spiritual guidance to develop our "goodness," and to work for peace and harmony instead of war and disunity.

For the cause of peace and development, let us hope that all our religious and political leaders will stretch out their hands in friendship to one another and to all people irrespective of caste or creed with a genuine feeling of love and brotherhood—to work for a peaceful world and all round development.

I strongly feel that the time has come for greater cohesion among our nations for building a more peaceful and secure world.

(Acharya Dr Lokesh Muni is Founder of Ahimsa Vishwa Bharti, India)

6

BUDDHARAKHITA

IN Buddhist philosophy, the name for physical world, *loka,* also refers to the physical and mental nature of human beings. Where many Western concepts consider man to be *in* the world, the Buddha's teachings consider human beings to be inseparable from the natural world. Much like a coin, human beings are separate from, but still a part of their larger environment. According to I. Ariyaratne[1] our environment is three-fold: Physical, mental, and social. Examples of our physical environment are well known—the flora and fauna, the surrounding terrain, climate, and other natural elements of the physical world. Our mental environment includes the conditions that either help or hinder intellectual, spiritual, religious, and ethical development. Finally, our social environment is defined by our relationship with other humans, as well as the larger community around us. Drawing from the ancient Buddhist commentaries, this paper explores the connection between preserving the environment and ecology, and understanding the five groups of natural laws[2]: Physical or inorganic laws; organic laws; moral laws; psychological laws and causal laws.

Utu Niyāma and *Bīja Niyāma*—Organic and Inorganic Physical Laws

The first two of the natural laws describe how physical things, including the four elements of fire, water, earth, and air, can interact. Things like climate, seasonal changes, natural disasters, and other purely physical systems fall into this category, along with the plant life that we depend on to survive. Together, these laws not only guide our physical environment, but also have a huge impact on our social and mental environments as well. Climate can affect the way people structure their communities and even influence our psychological health. Countries in colder, darker areas of the world often have much higher suicide rates. In addition, we depend heavily on environmental elements like the ozone layer that keeps us safe from harmful rays of the sun, or the forests that purify our air. While physical laws are only one part of the larger Buddhist understanding of the world, they are very important!

Physical laws are often the easiest to understand, but they also bring great suffering when ignored. When human beings exploit the natural world by irresponsible and dangerous practices like overfishing, deforestation, and environmental contamination, we break these laws. This often results in catastrophes like famine, drought, and irreversible ecological devastation.

Seeing man's ability to do great harm to the world, the Buddha offered wise advice for dealing with nature: '*Just as a bee gathers honey from the flower without injuring its color or fragrance, even so, the sage goes on his alms round in the village.*'[3] The bee needs the flower to make its food, and yet it does so without hurting the flower. In fact, the bee cross-pollinates the flower in the process; both the bee and the flower benefit. In the same way, human beings should earn their wealth without harming and exploiting the physical environment.

Kamma Niyāma—Moral Laws

Moral laws, sometimes referred to collectively as the law of *kamma* (or karma), are the laws that govern the potential results of our actions. Simply put, our *kamma* is the sum of all our actions. When we act in ways that hurt the world, we commit bad *kamma* and must deal with the results; when we act with kindness and wisdom, we generate good *kamma* and enjoy the benefits both in the present and future.

Selfishness and greed are unwholesome states of mind that lead to great suffering in our world. When we act out these desires, we bring great unwholesome *kamma* to ourselves. When we see our lakes and rivers polluted, and our forests burned down, that is due to our past *kamma*—the actions we took to contaminate and destroy. Civil war, ethnic conflict, and even genocide are all horribly negative actions, and the *kamma* that comes from them is terrible. Many innocent civilians have lost their lives and property because of ignorant people acting in ways that produce terrible, terrible *kamma*. Racism, intolerance, bigotry, and fundamentalism are all caused by ignorant and unwholesome mind states; those who engage in them reap terrible suffering for themselves and others.

However, when we resolve to act in ethical ways, we enjoy a peace that follows us like a shadow. Generosity, universal compassion, and wisdom all lead to skillful action, which in turn bring us great *kamma*. The responsible use of resources is good *kamma* for us and all beings, and we all enjoy the results. If we understand the law of *kamma*, seeing it not as a fatalistic system of punishment and reward, but instead as a natural law that brings good results from good action and bad results from bad action, we can work together to behave in ways that are skillful and constructive.

Citta Niyāma—Psychological Laws

The Citta Niyāma are the laws that govern our minds, as opposed to our bodies. The processes of consciousness, sensation, thought, and focus are all governed by these laws, which help us comprehend and make sense of the outside world. The six senses[4]—sight, taste, touch, smell, sound, and mind—are linked to their respective sense objects; just like you need a match and a striking pad to make a flame, you need an object in the world and one of your senses to make sense-consciousness. From these contacts, all mental objects arise.

Understanding and respecting our psychological laws can create both superb mental health, as well as a healthy social environment. Those who fill their minds with thoughts of good will, generosity, kindness, and restraint, add a great deal of security and stability to their communities. According to M. Emoto,[5] positive thinking might even affect the formation of physical things like ice crystals!

Dhamma Niyāma—Causal Laws

The causal laws guide the interaction between all other laws, linking them in a complex web of co-dependent arising and ceasing. For example, cutting down forests may lead to the arising of poor air quality, which leads to the arising of sickness and discomfort. On the other hand, a kind deed towards a neighbor may lead to the arising of thoughts of kindness and compassion, which can in turn lead to the arising of a healthy and vibrant community. Through an understanding of the causal laws that guide our interaction with the world, we can come to act in wise and productive ways, always knowing the consequences of our action and working towards creating conditions for the rise of a safe and loving world.

The *Dhamma* itself is the natural law that links us with everything else that exists in the natural world. Because of this unending chain of cause and effect, we are not isolated beings independent from other people, but instead just small parts of a larger world in which the entirety of existence is reflected. Knowing this with wisdom and direct experience helps us treat our natural world with tender care, boundless loving-kindness, and deep compassion.

Conclusion

Having explored the organic, inorganic, moral, psychological, and causal laws and how they affect the universe and everything in it, connecting all things in a large web of cause and effect, it becomes abundantly clear that if we understand this truth deeply and directly, we can begin to act in ways that are in tune with these natural laws. If we are ever going to live in harmony with the natural world, we must banish our excessive greed and selfish desire and invite generosity, cooperation, and contentment (with what is suitable, available, and within our means). If we are ever going to create healthy and just societies, we must abandon hatred and cruelty and embrace universal love, tolerance, forgiveness, and compassion for all beings. And most importantly, if we are ever going to bring about spiritual growth and development in our individual hearts and minds, we must cast out our ignorance and delusion and realize the truth of our own interconnectedness. Through our universal responsibility, we can save our planet, heal our communities, and transform our minds.

I will end with a short saying. 'Just take the h in 'heart' and move it to the end. You'll get Earth.' Our heart is connected to our Earth! Let us protect our Mother Nature and preserve her as we would preserve the most precious part of our bodies, the heart. It is not too late. The best time to take action is now! And the next best time is now. You and I are responsible for the destiny of our Mother Earth, the whole Planet and for creating a world of compassion and wisdom.

(Ven Buddharakhita is Founder & Abbot, Uganda Buddhist Centre, Entebbe, Uganda)

REFERENCES

1 Suvimalee, Bhikkhuni, Wie Ming, Iromi Ariyaratne, and Hasanthi Dahayake. *Sri Lanka International Journal of Buddhist Studies*. Vol. 1. Kandy: SIBA-DCI Research Centre, 2010. p. 240.

2 *The Atthsālinī: Buddhaghosa's Commentary on the Dhammasaṅaṇi*. Ed. Edward Muller. London: The Pali Text Society, 1897. p. 272.
Imasmiṃ pana ṭhāne pañcavidhaniyāmaṃ nāma gaṇhiṃsu bījaniyāmaṃ utuniyāmaṃ kammaniyāmaṃ Dhammaniyāmaṃ cittaniyāma ti.

3 *The Dhammapada*. Trans. Achariya Buddharakkhita. Kandy: Buddhist Publication Society, 2007. (Verse 49, p. 33)

4 PTS: M.III.216
Saḷāyatana: (Saḷāyatanavibhaṅga suttaṃ MN 137)
cakkhāyatanaṃ sotāyatanaṃ ghānāyatanaṃ jivhāyatanaṃ kāyāyatanaṃ manāyatanaṃ.
Give rise to:
rūpāyatanaṃ saddāyatanaṃ gandhāyatanaṃ rasāyatanaṃ phoṭṭhabbāyatanaṃ dhammāyatanaṃ

5 Emoto, Masaru. *The Hidden Message in Water*. Oregon: Beyond Words Publications, 2004. p. 4.

Primary Sources

The Dhammapada. Trans. Achariya Buddharakkhita. Kandy: Buddhist Publication Society, 2007.

The Atthsālinī: Buddhaghosa's Commentary on the Dhammasaṅaṇi. Ed. Edward Muller. London: The Pali Text Society, 1897.

Secondary Sources

Emoto, Masaru. *The Hidden Message in Water*. Oregon: Beyond Words Publications, 2004.

Suvimalee, Bhikkhuni, Wie Ming, Iromi Ariyaratne, and Hasanthi Dahayake. *Sri Lanka International Journal of Buddhist Studies*. Vol. 1. Kandy: SIBA-DCI Research Centre, 2010.

Zangpo, Shebphen, and Francis Huang. *Sangha Talk English Conversation Textbook for the Buddhist Sangha*. Taiwan: the Corporate Body of the Buddha Educational Foundation, 2002.

7

NARESH MAN BAJRACHARYA

A conference titled "Samvad", held in September 2015, in New Delhi, India was a thoughtful, path breaking and milestone event that established a common understanding on the need for a paradigm shift from Conflict Resolution to Conflict Avoidance, and from Environmental Regulation to Environmental Consciousness. The conference emphasized on the theory "prevention is better than cure". Once again, I would like to express my sincere thanks to all who contributed in Samvad.

For the second edition of Samvad, this time we are in Yangon, Myanmar, with the theme "*Dialogue for Peace, Harmony and Security—A Global Initiative for Conflict Avoidance and Environment Consciousness*". This theme is an upgrade of the last conference and relevant without doubt. The concept note on the theme is very clear and meaningful. It focuses on the need of a dialogue among religions and between the spirituals masters of various religions to establish peace, harmony and security in the world. This dialogue would play a vital role in the global initiative for conflict avoidance and environment consciousness. I would like to congratulate the organizing committee for organizing Samvad II and I wish it a grand success.

I would like to commence my short speech with the quotation from the concept note for this Samvad as follows:

> "...peace among nations is not possible without peace among religions, peace among religions is not possible without dialogue among religions and dialogue among religions is impossible without investigating the fundamentals of different religions..."

Although very well said, the first statement of this sentence "*peace among nations is not possible without peace among religions*" is not necessarily true in all situations. According to this statement, countries are facing conflict or turmoil due to lack of cohesion amongst religions, hence religion is the obstacle towards peace in a country, religion is the cause of turmoil in a country.

In this regard, first we need to investigate the reality of the first statement, we need to study and discuss on that motion. Is it the case in all countries facing turmoil?

From my experience rather than the study, the statement "*peace among nations is not possible without peace among religions*" is only partially true in case of the countries where there are religious conflicts. But there are many countries where there are no religious conflicts but people still lead painful lives having no peace. Nepal is one such country where there is no religious conflict, but from the beginning of modern history, people of Nepal have been suffering. During 104 years of Rana autocratic period, the handful of autocratic Rana rulers enjoyed optimum privileges while the rest of subjects were unduly exploited economically and dominated politically without having basic humanitarian rights. Hence, this compelled people to move against the autocratic regime and they sacrificed themselves eventually succeeding in introducing democracy in Nepal. The people have now experienced peace and relief to some extent. I learned of these things through studying the history of Nepal. In my youth, majority of people suffered due to the mono-linguistic, mono-religious, mono-cultural policy of the ruling party that stood against freedom of speech and people's sovereignty. The people of Nepal suffered for a long time due to politics, and as a consequence they had restless lives. In Nepal, this plight was not a consequence of conflicts among the religions. Whatever conflicts and sufferings that people underwent during that period were in fact the result of political instability and hindered relations with neighboring countries, that still exist. Hence, generalizing that turmoil or conflicts in the world is the consequence of religious conflict is beyond the reality.

Now, let us change the context! There is no doubt a need for dialogue to resolve any problems. Dialogue is different from debate[1] and discussion. Dialogue is not simply a way of conversation. Dialogue is a medium that helps to resolve doubts, dilemmas and controversies by investigating realities and facts. It minimizes the gap between conflicting parties by bringing up common points of compromise, and developing understanding and trustworthiness between them. In other words, a dialogue identifies the actual problem, finds out the root cause of the problem, generates potential solution of the problem, and provides the way out of it as well.[2]

There are not only incidences of successful dialogues[3] but also ample examples of failure attempt as well that resulted in escalating the conflicts further. It must be due of nature of dialogue; in fact, the dialogue must be a "Samyak Samvad" (Right Dialogue).

In this context, it is worth citing the dialogue between Bhikshu Nagasena and the King Milinda as mentioned in the Buddhist text the Milindapanha (the question of King Milinda) of 1st century AD. According to the text, King Milinda expressed his desire to have a dialogue with Bhikshu Nagasena. In response to the King, Bhikshu Nagasena said that he was not interested to have "Rajavada" (Royal Dialogue) rather he would prefer to have "Panditavada" (Scholarly Dialogue). Then King Milinda agreed to follow the Scholarly Dialogue. It was only then, that they entered into a dialogue.

According to Bhikshu Nagasena, the Royal Dialogue is such a dialogue in which position, authority or power holder has unilateral dominance over the inferior, subordinate and powerless opponent. The dominant party expects whatever he says to be unconditionally accepted or followed without failure by the opponent. In case of failure to follow what, the dominant party said, the opponent may be penalized accordingly. In such a dialogue the former party dominates the later who has no option except to obey what the former says.

According to Bhikshu Nagasena, the scholarly dialogue is one where there is no discrimination between the parties involved. Either on the basis of their status or power but there's only mutual respect and coherence. The dialogue is based solely on logic and reasoning, with no feelings of regret on being defeated in the motion, instead there's respect towards the opponent's opinion. There's due acknowledgment and gratification on knowing the reality.

Scholarly dialogue is conducted in righteous way, so it's not exaggeration to call it as "Right Dialogue". In modern context, a right dialogue could be defined as one in which there is:

- two or more parties involved;
- respect towards each other as equal entities;

- equal status—no discrimination of any kind;
- nothing to do with winning or losing the game;
- aim of reaching the truth and reality;
- focus on result oriented problem-solving;
- arguments not based on faith, but reasoning or logic;
- no negative feelings regardless of the outcome, instead there's a feeling of contentment from getting enlightened and eliminating ignorance by acquiring true knowledge;
- expression of gratitude towards each other, and a commitment to follow what is agreed.

Such type of Right Dialogue will certainly contribute in a global initiative for Conflict Avoidance and Environment Consciousness that would ultimately cause Peace, Harmony and Security in the globe.

(Prof. Naresh Man Bajracharya is Vice Chancellor, Lumbini Buddhist University, Nepal.)

REFERENCES

1 While debate and controversy have been the norms, an increasingly diverse and conflicted world calls us to collaborate with one another in order to survive and share the planet as one humanity. Many forward thinking citizens of the world now realize that in order to create just and humane societies, all kinds of individuals and groups need to come together to talk about the important and controversial matters that affect their survival and progress. They are also aware that how we talk is important—dialogue must address issues of equity before it can be successful.

2 Webster defines the purpose of dialogue as "seeking mutual understanding and harmony." In philosopher Martin Buber's classic work *I and Thou,* Buber suggests that in authentic dialogue something far deeper than ordinary conversation goes on. Dialogue is a process of successful relationship building.

3 Example of successful Dialogue in history:

a) Dialogue played a special role in reversing the nuclear arms race and ending the Cold War. Some years after the end of Ronald Reagan's presidency, George Shultz, who had been Reagan's Secretary of State, asked Mikhail Gorbachev, former president of the Soviet Union, what the turning point in the Cold War had been.
"Reykjavík," Gorbachev answered unhesitatingly.
He explained that at their meeting in Reykjavík, Iceland, he and Ronald Reagan had for the first time entered into genuine dialogue with each other—a dialogue that extended far beyond their main agenda (arms control) to cover their values, assumptions, and aspirations for their two nations. Gorbachev credited this dialogue with establishing enough trust and mutual understanding to begin to reverse the nuclear arms race.

b) In Oslo, Norway, in the year before Israel's Prime Minister, Yitzhak Rabin, was assassinated, a delegation of top-level Israelis and Palestinians, previously implacable enemies, held nonstop dialogue sessions over a period of months. Together they hammered out a blueprint for peace in the Middle East that lasted until Rabin's violent death upset the political balance.

c) In San Diego County, a group of American and Mexican businesspeople and community leaders convene regularly under the auspices of San Diego Dialogue, a project of the University of California at San Diego (UCSD). These dialogues are so successful that once-intractable border and regional problems are now dealt with almost routinely.(1999 New York Times Company)

***

DIALOGUE BETWEEN KING MILINDA AND MONK NAGASENA

The King Said: 'Reverend Sir, will you discuss with me again?'

Bhikshu (Monk) Nagasena Replied: 'If your Majesty will discuss as a scholar *(Pandit)* well; but if you will discuss as a king, no.'

The King: 'How is it then that scholars discuss?'

The Bhikshu: 'When scholars talk a matter over one with another then is there a winding up, an unravelling; one or other is convicted of error, and he then acknowledges his mistake; distinctions are drawn, and contra-distinctions; and yet there by they are not angered. Thus do scholars, O king, discuss.'

The King: 'And how do Kings discuss?'

The Bhikshu: 'When a king your Majesty, discusses a matter, and he advances a point, if any one differ from him on that point, he is apt to fine him, saying: "Inflict such and such a punishment upon that fellow!" Thus, your Majesty, do kings discuss.'

The King: 'Very well, It is as a scholar, not as a King, that I will discuss. Let your reverence talk unrestrainedly, as you would with a brother, or a novice, or a lay disciple, or even with a servant. Be not afraid!'

The Bhikshu Nagasena said with thankfulness: 'Very good, your Majesty.'

(Source: T.W. Rhys Davids (Trans.), The Question of King Milinda, Part I, Low Price Publications, Delhi, 1996, pp.46-47)

8

CHIDANAND SARASWATI

ACCORDING to Hinduism, the core tenet, the core teaching states, "*Ayam nijah paroveti ganana laghuchetasam, udaracharitanantu vasudhaiva kutumbakam.*" *Vasudhaiva Kutumbakam*—the whole world is one family. In this family, not only human beings but all living beings are also integral part of the collective whole. The Isha Upanishad starts with the verse, "*Ishavasyam idam sarvam. yat kincha jagatyam jagat. Tena tyaktena bhunjitha. ma gridhah kasya svid dhanam,*" which states that the Divine is not only omnipresent and omnipotent but pervades all of creation. Hence, Hindu culture is not a culture of mere tolerance but it is one of acceptance, it is a celebration of unity amidst diversity.

One of the keys to this culture of acceptance and oneness is the understanding that we may worship our own but we must respect all. Another important key is a beautiful mantra "*Aano bhadra krtavo yantu vishwatah*"—let all the noble thoughts come from all directions. These two mantras set the foundation for interfaith dialogue as the key and the solution to peaceful and sustainable world for all.

India is a country where these values are intimately intertwined with its culture and history. It is the world's largest democracy wherein all major faith traditions have co-existed in harmony and unity for decades.

As HH the Dalai Lama said recently, "As India develops and grows there is much to be proud of. It pleases me to see that the international community is becoming ever more aware of India's importance, not only because it is the world's largest democratic nation, but also because of its exemplary traditions of religious harmony, *karuna* and ahimsa. As our world becomes increasingly interdependent, I look forward to seeing India take a more active role on every continent, sharing these treasures for the greater good."

I am glad therefore that so many eminent leaders from India are gathered here today in Myanmar, our neighbor and our friend, as we discuss these common human values, especially the values of karuna and ahimsa which form the very core of Hindu and Buddhist traditions. These are so greatly needed today, especially in the face of increasing conflict, violence, sectarianism, depleting natural resources and climate change.

Lastly, our cultures have always lauded *samvad* (dialogue) and today I would like to also share that there is a beautiful connection between *samvad* and *samvedana. Samvad* (dialogue) helps us break the illusory borders and boundaries of separation, of us vs them. Through dialogue we begin to move from a focus on differences to a shift towards our similarities and commonalities, discovering there is indeed more that unites us than separates us. Hence, our sense of Self is expanded through *Samvad* and we begin to be at a place where *samvedana* or deep connection and sensitivity for "the perceived other" can be experienced. In this space we don't only sympathize but can truly empathize, our inherent nature becomes one of compassion and love and not of separation and isolation.

Today let us pledge to take the *yatra* from *Samvad* to *samvedana,* from mere resolution and declaration to action and commitment. Let each one of us pledge to concrete steps and actions, within our communities and congregations, to be the change we want to see in the world.

I personally commit through the Global Interfaith WASH Alliance. We will continue bringing the interfaith leaders and communities together to improve water, sanitation and hygiene (WASH) for everyone everywhere and through GIWA's World Toilet College we will continue to engage and empower communities and congregations to demand, supply, maintain and sustain the change towards improved WASH.

Through the Ganga Action Parivar we will encourage all communities to see our work for River Ganga as a symbol for all rivers and water bodies around the world, as the need to act to protect our natural resources is vital to our individual and collective futures. We will continue to encourage mass tree plantation, increase awareness and education on water conservation and river's/ Nature's rights, promoting green technologies and encouraging people to not merely wait for solutions and laws but to be the solution, transforming challenges into opportunities.

Through Divine Shakti Foundation we will continue to deepen the connection and thereby the solutions for preserving and protecting the divine feminine in all its forms, both in the Shakti and the Prakriti, because Hinduism teaches us that there is an inherent and intricate link between the divine feminine—in the form of our mothers and sisters—and all of Mother Nature. Hence, protecting one is linked and essential to protecting the other. Thereby encouraging women to come forward to lead the change.

Hence, let us all raise our hands and join them with the person next to us in a pledge to work collectively and work individually to be the peace, the green and sustainable change we wish to see in the world.

(Swami Chidanand Saraswati is President & Spiritual Head, Parmarth Niketan Ashram, Rishikesh, India)

9

MADHAVPRIYADAS

WE are here to discover the right way for peace, harmony and security through religion. It can be found only and only by achieving the consciousness, that is the core of all religions.

State of being conscious, being aware, is all pervasive, ever peaceful, harmonious and secure. Consciousness is present everywhere, in all living beings and non-living things. That is why we respect and worship trees and plants in Hinduism.

Ram, Krishna, Tathagata Buddha, Sankaracharya, Mahatma Gandhi and Prophets of the world were full of consciousness, this state of being conscious enabled them to change the world.

The catch is that though the consciousness is ever present, it is still hidden. We need to find the right path to attain it.

Once I went to an assembly. There was too much noise. I noticed that the cause of noise were the volunteers. I requested them to be quiet. As they became quiet, the whole assembly became quiet.

Similarly, the religious leaders are also like volunteers. If they are cool, calm and respectful, there is peace everywhere.

Attaining consciousness with the path of spirituality is our goal but we are worshipping the instruments, the means and our establishments. This results into a struggle as we are not sincere about our goal.

Somewhat the religious leaders are answerable for this conflict between choosing the righteous path and adoring false establishments. The difficult journey to achieve consciousness begins with being respectful to each other.

(Swami Madhavpriyadas is Representative of Hindu Dharma Acharya Mahasabha, India and President of SGVP, Ahmedabad, India)

10

MAHN PALMERSTON

IN today's age of Information Technology, with tremendous communication capability, the world has become a small village because of information technology. At the same time, we face cruel conflicts and wars around us every day as well. While technologically, we are live in IT age, brutal events in the world prove that people are treating each other worse than Stone Age. As we approach an age of advanced technology, we have to accept the existence of a mindset of brutality on the other side.

Religion is the one that provides instructions and guidelines on how to live peacefully and become cultivated people. The purpose of religion is to teach human beings and show the significance of sharing a tender, loving, kind, and well-mannered relationship with people of each religion. Four religions (Christianity, Hindu, Islam and Buddhism) have taught people valuable wisdoms over thousand years and their respective practitioners have handed over core essence of this wisdom generations over generations. Nevertheless, it is peculiar that brutal and inhumane events such as wars, conflicts are still happen in the world, despite these teachings.

For me, I trust in centuries old world religions which contain endless meanings and great values because of their own sacred books like Vedas, Tripitaka, Bible & Quran, etc. I trust all these religions will never fade away because they have existed before our birth, and it will exist after our death. Then, I love to learn all sacred works, all Holy books, for obtaining inner peace. I love to practice what I learned.

I love to share the fruits which I gained from these practices.

I love to involve in the discussion with Venerable Sayadaws and Sacred Leaders and get new ideas about the sacred words. I love to encourage promoting all these sacred religions for sustainable peace.

In conclusion, I honestly urge all of you to shake hands together for promotion of peace that every creature needs. According to U Thant, former Secretary General of UN (1961-1971): "We are to promote world religions if we want Sustainable Peace."

(Mahn Palmerston is General Secretary, Myanmar Council of Churches, Yangon)

SUMMATION

1

NC Vij

IN Sep 2015 during the first Samvad conference in New Delhi, which was inaugurated by our Hon Prime Minister Shri Narendra Modi, VIF had the pleasure of hosting over 200 extraordinarily intelligent minds from all over the world discussing and debating, as to how to create a more peaceful world. We were particularly blessed by the presence and benediction by Most Venerable Sitagu Sayadaw Dr Ashin Nyanissara.

Let me say that SAMVAD II has been an equally gratifying experience. It is with immense satisfaction that I stand here to share with you the happenings of the last 48 hours. Let me also state that it is not possible to recount from all the presentations made. So those who I miss out will have to forgive me for that. Let me also say that their contributions were equally meritorious.

SAMVAD aims to initiate a lot of intermingling, free transmissions and exchanges among religions, scholars and institutions towards building a new infrastructure and eco-system. This is with a view to take the SAMVAD initiative to the grassroots and in the global discourse as a movement for humankind to the idea of peaceful co-existence amongst fellow human beings and nature. Our spiritual masters have a major responsibility in steering us towards this mission. We do hope that post SAMVAD II this process of cross transmission and easy intermingling will gather momentum.

I will now like to recall some of the major aspects that have emerged during these two days.

Day One

The video speeches of Prime Minister Narendra Modi and Prime Minster Shinzo Abe, the inspiring speeches by Most Venerable Sayadaw Dr. Ashin Nyanissara ji, His Excellency the Governor of Uttar Pradesh, India, Shri Ram Naik, the Honourable Minister for Religious Affairs, Govt of Myanmar, Mr. Thura U Aung Ko and the special address by Mr U Theung Tun, National Security Advisor to Her Excellency State Councillor Daw Aung San Suu Kyi set the ball rolling. Their speeches underlined the emerging dangers to the world peace and environmental catastrophe looming over our Mother Earth, the only home for the mankind.

In his speech, the Hon Prime Minister of India. Shri Narendra Modi referred to critical questions world is facing today. Questions about global challenges like conflicts and climate change, what lessons do Asian values and democracy hold for the world today, how to live in peace and harmony and secure our lives are not only deeply philosophical but also crucial to our contemporary world. He stressed that "it is only through deep and prolonged dialogue—Samvad—that we may discover hidden synergies, resolving contradictions and ways to cut though deep rooted religious stereotypes, prejudices that divide communities across the world and sow seeds of conflicts". Terming climate change as nature's reaction to man's disrespect of nature he referred to Hindu Buddhist philosophical approach of living in harmony with nature and the need for revering nature rather than just seeing it as a resource to exploit.

The Hon Prime Minister of Japan Mr Shinzo Abe in his speech said that in Asia people have pursued various thoughts and religions from ancient times. Referring to Buddha's famous words "May all living beings be happy" as spirit of tolerance and compassion that appeals coexistence of all lives, he termed this belief as flowing from the source to the rivers of Asian values that has supported diversity and flourishing of democracy in Asia.

Shri Gurumurthy from India, and Professor Dr Khin Maung Nyunt from Myanmar, very eloquently set the agenda for the two days of deliberations to evolve a new paradigm of philosophical approach to these issues and the need for taking the initiative to the grass roots. Spiritual masters were requested to take the lead where the political leaders have failed. Thus the spiritual leaders from all faiths, who were present in the conference, carry a huge responsibility.

Both the illustrious speakers referred to religions as sources of both conflicts and peace depending on its interpretations and exploitation by vested interests.

Mr. Gurumurthy quoted from the Roman Catholic theologian Hans Kungs who had said, *that peace among nations is not possible without peace among religions, peace among religions is not possible without dialogue among religions and dialogue among religions is impossible without investigating the fundamentals of different religions.* Thus open and transparent philosophic dialogue, which is inherent in Asiatic traditions, should form the core of conflict avoidance paradigm and the two great religions—Hinduism and Buddhism should take the lead.

They stressed on the need to break the shackles of ideologies and strive for philosophical debate as a means to develop universal understanding. Further, in a world which seems to be running short of ideas, other than government actions, the conference seeks to open people-participatory approach by going back to fundamentals of our spiritual discourse. This will mean Environment Consciousness and shifting from exploitation towards respect and harmony with nature.

The Round Table Summit of the Spiritual Masters, participated by most eminent Spiritual Masters of Buddhism, Hinduism, Islam, Christianity, Sikhism and Jainism provided some clear directions to us on:-

a) Creating a conducive and compelling eco-system with the objective of emphasizing the importance of dialogue and understanding for avoiding conflicts

b) Instituting sustainable institutional model for frank and open dialogues between non-conflicting philosophies, ideologies and evolving a long-term perspective for promoting institutions to carry forward ideas generated though these dialogues for lasting peace, harmony and security

c) Bringing environment consciousness in global discourse and promoting significant changes in the way our present economic system is structured which is in conflict with nature and is thus unsustainable

d) Establishing a global network of leaders in a wide range of social, political, environmental and intellectual arena committed to the promotion of democratic values, conflict avoidance, environmental consciousness, universal responsibility and ethical behaviors

The proceedings and discussion in both the Round Table Summits and the Academic Sessions on both days showed that there was total consensus on the aforesaid approach.

The speakers of the Academic session on Day 1 presented their views on the theme of Evolving a Non-Conflicting Philosophical Paradigm for Conflict Avoidance, Peace & Harmony.

Speaker after speaker stressed on the principle of everyone having freedom of practicing their own religion without any interference from others. As a matter of fact it is only when certain radicalized elements try to force their own ideologies on others, that it becomes a major reason for strife. The speakers also emphasised on the importance of dialogue and the capacity to listen to the alternate viewpoints. They stressed on the need for adopting non-conflicting ideologies and agreed that this conclave offered great opportunity to analyze the threats and challenges to the maintenance of world peace and tranquility and also suggesting sustainable approaches.

Day 2

Now I come to the proceedings of Day 2. The deliberations at the Round Table Summit of Spiritual Masters focussed on evolving a consensus on Action Plan and creating institutional means to take the Samvad initiative to grassroots and sustainable eco system.

The Academic session on Day 2 was on the theme of Environmental Consciousness. The eminent speakers were engaged in a spirited and composite dialogue on environmental consciousness being the prime paradigm of socio-cultural cooperation and collective global action. The philosophical underpinning of *dharma* was also touched upon by many speakers Environmental protection would be possible only with self-awareness based on our ancient religious beliefs with respect to Mother Earth.

It was pointed out that the Earth is our only home in this universe, which we have been taking for granted and we easily forget that we are part of nature and depend on it for our life. We have scarred the Earth and polluted its environment, poisoned the very air we breathe and water we drink and leading the world to another mass extinction of animal and plant species.

Hon Minister of State for Home Affairs, Govt of India, Sh. Kiren Rijiju in his speech called for an urgent need to mobilise a mass movement to create awareness on what crisis planet earth and humans are facing and to bring Environment Consciousness in global political, religious, social and public discourse.

The rich and scholarly discourse, research and frank opinions expressed by all the speakers and delegates in the academic sessions on Days 1 and 2 on the theme of Conflict Resolution and Environment Consciousness, will certainly help us to take this initiative further.

Conclusion

World today is in a new phase of uncertainty and danger emanating from galloping religious and ideological conflicts which increasingly find expression through barbaric terrorism and massive sectarian violence, within and outside the ideological societies. The situation calls for innovative, non-formal and strategic efforts to handle these new and emerging challenges.

The speeches by our esteemed Guest of Honours and deliberations at both the Round Table Summit and the Academic Sessions is a clear indicator that the intelligentsia and religious and spiritual gurus are completely aligned with this thought process in letter and spirit.

There was an overwhelming consensus among all the participants that in this age of conflict based on religious and ideological rivalries, shrinking natural resources and looming environmental catastrophe, there is an urgent need to find an alternate narrative to issues and crises confronting human civilization.

The conference not only met the objectives that we set out to achieve but has also gone much beyond that. We must build on this momentum.

Now, when we have come to the last phase of this conclave, let me say that this marks the beginning of a continued process which will ultimately lead to global peace, harmony, security and environment consciousness. This is our earnest hope.

We welcome the announcement by the President of the Japan Foundation that the next conference would be held in Tokyo in 2018. I too wish to join him in announcing the next edition of Samvad III by us will be in 2019. The venue will be decided in due course.

We are particularly fortunate to have the gracious presence of Hon. Chief Minister of Uttar Pradesh, India, Mahant Yogi Adityanath ji at this valedictory session. He is one of our longest serving illustrious parliamentarians, 25 years in parliament, and now is the Chief Minister of the largest and most populous state of India—Uttar Pradesh.

Hope cross-transmission amongst various religions will intensify.

(General NC Vij is Former Chief of Indian Army. He was Director VIF from 2014–2017)

2

ASHIN NYANISSARA

THE Interfaith Dialogue for Peace, Harmony and Security, jointly organised by the Sitagu International Buddhist Missionary Association, the Vivekananda International Foundation (VIF) and the Myanmar Institute of Strategic and International Studies (MISIS), in association with the Japan Foundation, is nearing an end.

This great and grand conference has been an enormous success, thanks to your collective efforts and the invaluable contribution of distinguished spiritual leaders from different faiths; keynote speakers; eminent scholars; panelists and enthusiastic participants. All have worked towards global peace and security during our two-day conference.

I would particularly like to thank H.E. Narendra Modi, Prime Minister of India and H.E. Shinzo Abe, Prime Minister of Japan, for their video recorded messages. My thanks also to H.E. Thura U Aung Ko, Union Minister for Religious Affairs and Culture, Government of the Republic of the Union of Myanmar; H.E. U Thaung Tun, National Security Advisor of the Republic of the Union of Myanmar; H.E. Shri Mahant Yogi Adityanath, Honourable Chief Minister of Uttar Pradesh; H.E. Shri Ram Naik, Governor of Uttar Pradesh; H.E. U Phyo Min Thein, Chief Minister of Yangon Region; H.E. Mr. Nobuo Kishi, State Minister for Foreign Affairs of Japan; Honourable H.R.S.D. Mitrapala, Deputy Minister of Buddhasasana and Justice of Sri Lanka; H.E. Mr. Kiren Rijiju, Honourable Minister of State for Home Affairs of India; H.E. U Naing Ngan Linn, Minister for Social Affairs of the Government of Yangon Region for gracing this conference with their presence and remarks at the inaugural and closing sessions. My special thanks also go to the co-chairs who moderated the two sessions of the conference. I would also like to thank the officials and staff members of the Ministry of Religious Affairs and Culture, Ministry of Foreign Affairs and Ministry of Home Affairs, members of the management committee, working committee of Sitagu International Buddhist Missionary Association and especially, the chief donors, the President of the Htoo Foundation and officials and staff members of the Kandawgyi Palace Hotel, for providing accommodation and meals for the guests, the President of Kan Baw Za Banks Group who arranged the free air travel to and from Bagan, the Skynet Buddha TV Channel and all the volunteers, for their valuable support and countless hours of service, without which, this conference could not have been such a resounding success.

Over 100 representatives from 30 countries participated in this conference. More than 100 messages and papers were presented in the parallel sessions, A and B. Despite different views and perspectives, there was convergence on the need to find a common platform and common ground, to maintain world peace and security.

However, we still have to work a lot more in the future. I'm confident that frequent discussions and meetings of this kind will ensure better results in our collaborative efforts, to promote peace in the world.

After the conclusion of this Interfaith Dialogue, you will pay a visit to the majestic Shwedagon Pagoda, the most unique religious symbol of Myanmar. Tomorrow, we have arranged a day trip to Bagan, the cultural heartland of Myanmar. With more than 2,000 temples located in 16 square miles, it is the richest archaeological site in Southeast Asia. Bagan flourished between the 11th-13th century and it is the site of the best of Myanmar's architecture, including sculptures and murals. After returning from Bagan you all will prepare for your journey back home.

Again, I thank each of you for your participation, and the noble spirit of universal brotherhood, which will promote our endeavours for world peace, harmony and security.

May I now conclude with my ardent wish that may:

- Members of different faiths build up mutual understanding and respect among each other

- Members of different faiths live together in peace, refraining from interfering in matters of other faiths
- Members of different faiths enjoy peaceful co-existence by exercising, great tolerance.

(Dr Ashin Nyanissara is the Most Venerable Sitagu Sayadaw, Sitagu International Buddhist Academy, Yangon)

3

U Phyo Min Thein

IT gives me great pleasure to give this closing speech at Samvad II, the Interfaith Dialogue for Peace, harmony and Security of the World.

I am sure you have had fruitful discussions during the last two days, on two very important topics: Conflict Avoidance; and Environment Consciousness. I also hope you have had a chance to enjoy the beautiful sights of Yangon city.

Since assuming my duties as Chief Minister of Yangon Region, I have tried my best to make the City of Yangon not only a pleasant place to live and work, but also to upgrade the city transportation service and municipal services. I also know that it is very important for the citizens of Yangon to live in harmony and peace with each other. That is why I am very much interested in the successful outcome of this conference.

As you may all know, the citizens of Yangon Region all have very high expectations. They wish to see very significant changes as soon as possible. On this point I wish to remind them that every government has to carry over all the good and bad actions of their predecessors. I wish to reassure them that all the ministers in the cabinet of the Yangon Regional Government, are working to the best of their abilities with full *cetana* to make the City of Yangon not only the commercial hub of Myanmar with all the modern facilities, but also one of the premier tourist centres of the country.

In our efforts to turn the Yangon region into a green and beautiful city, I wish to take this opportunity to request the citizens of Yangon region to be aware of their duties as citizens. On our part, I have given instructions to the

YCDC—Yangon City Development Committee, to keep all our parks and streets clean, safe and green.

In addition, I have taken note of the fact that after every heavy downpour, many of our streets get flooded, which leads to traffic jams. The fact of the matter is that when we assumed our duties as the new regional government, we inherited a city which had many blocked drains and too many cars. Although it may be quite easy to criticise, it takes time to untangle this mess. We have started tackling this problem by overhauling the city transportation system and cleaning up the blocked drains of the whole city. We promise to do our part, but I also wish to request the citizens of Yangon city to keep the city clean and beautiful by not throwing garbage into the drains and litter on to the pavements and streets.

Let me now turn to the two main themes of this conference: Conflict Avoidance and Environment Consciousness. The City of Yangon is home to citizens of many races and religious faiths. We have many religious communities living side by side with Buddhists. If you go around the city you will see mosques, Hindu temples and churches right in the heart of the city. Throughout the history of our country, the citizens of Yangon have lived in peace and harmony respecting each other and the religious beliefs of others.

I wish to inform this august gathering of spiritual masters and scholars from many countries in the region that we the Myanmar people are very generous, courteous and tolerant. That is what our Buddhist teachings teach us. We are taught to treat others as fellow human beings and not discriminate on the basis of religion or race. We are taught to be humble and to practice loving kindness or *metta.*

As chief minister of the Yangon Regional Government, it is my duty to ensure that all the citizens live in peace and harmony. That is why I think that this conference, which has focused on peace, harmony and security in the World, is important, not only for our region, but the whole of Myanmar.

Yangon City and the Yangon Region have the great privilege of having very important and holy places of worship such as the Golden Shwedagon Pagoda, the Sule Pagoda in the city centre, the Botahtaung Pagoda and the Gabar Aye Pagoda, to name just a few. These are holy places of worship as well as important tourist sites.

In this day and age when the scourge of religious extremism is on the rise, it has become the responsibility of our regional government to keep all these religious edifices safe and secure. Our duty is not only to keep the Buddhist places of worship safe and secure, but all places of worship safe. This means mosques, Hindu temples and any other place of worship.

Therefore, on behalf of the Regional Government of Yangon, I wish to express my unqualified support for the points raised in the Declaration issued today. May I wish all of you a safe and pleasant journey home. I hope your short stay in Yangon has been a pleasant one and I want to urge you all to come back again as tourists to visit other parts of Myanmar.

I thank the organisers of this conference for choosing Yangon City as the venue for this very important conference.

(Mr U Phyo Min Thein is the Chief Minister of Yangon Region, Myanmar)

4

Yogi Adityanath

I am very happy to be here for, 'Samvad II: Dialogue for Peace, Harmony and Security—a Global Initiative for Consciousness'. I also feel greatly honoured and humbled to be able to share my thoughts with this august gathering of spiritual leaders, eminent philosophers and scholars besides other.

The first programme of this series that was held in New Delhi on September 03, and 04, 2015, was graced by the Hon'ble Prime Minister of India, Sri Narendra Modi ji himself.

Close on the heels of that programme, the Hon'ble Prime Minister while speaking at a Buddhist Conclave held on September 05, 2015 at Bodhgaya, had said that conflict avoidance and environmental conservation are possible if we follow the tenets of Buddhist philosophy.

I am overwhelmed by a host of emotions to be just standing on the pious soil of Myanmar. Myanmar is a land which has always reverberated in our minds as 'Brahmadesh' which is so close to the hearts of the Indians. Our citizens have always been united in mind and spirit by a common approach to *Dhamma*, i.e. religion, also termed *Dharma*. I want to illustrate this by recounting an anecdote that shows how our destinies have been inter-linked for a long-long time.

We are all aware of how emperor Thibon was dethroned and sent to exile in Ratnagiri, a small town on the western coast of India.

Many of us may not know that almost a year later, a great leader of the Indian Freedom struggle, Lokmanya Bal Ganga Dhar Tilak was banished by the same colonial rulers from his motherland, and confined in Mandalay Jail.

Perhaps, it is a coincidence that Lokmanya Tilak authored his seminal work, *Geeta Rahasya* while he in captivity in Mandalay. This great work of Tilak Maharaj is a critique of *Karmayoga,* which is *Srimad Bhagavad Geeta's* foremost principle.

Karmayoga or *Karma Marga,* in Hinduism is the spiritual path, which lays great emphasis on right action, at the right moment, by relinquishing all material desires. Self-realisation, in keeping with the principles of the Geeta, is the ultimate goal. Incidentally, who other than the Tathagata, whom we Hindus worship as Lord Buddha, could be a better guide to lead us all the path of knowledge and enlightenment?

As a Hindu, and as an Indian, I am indebted to this land, where this great spiritual treatise was composed.

The three seminal teachings of Lord Buddha are: *Sharanam Gachchhami; Dhammam Sharanam Gachchhami*; and *Sangham Sharanam Gachchhami.* They ushered in the much desired change in the old Indian society and I am convinced they are much more relevant today, for providing a healing touch to the people all over the world.

It is a matter of great pride for Uttar Pradesh, to which I belong, that several important places connected with the life of Lord Buddha are located sit there. Lord Buddha delivered His first sermon at Sarnath near Varanasi. The *Mahaparinirvana Sthal* of the Buddha is at Kushinagar. Many more sacred places linked to the life of Tathagata such as Shravasti, Kapilvastu, Kaushambi, Sankisaetal are also located in our state. Lumbini, the birth place of Lord Buddha, and his *Tapasya Sthali* (place of penance and meditation) i.e. Bodhgaya, are also not far from Uttar Pradesh.

The task of connecting different places related to Lord Buddha is underway in Uttar Pradesh. This will enable international tourists and devotees to reach these places with ease, for an unmatched spiritual experience.

I am a Sanyasi of the Nath sect, which is an excellent example of the composite Hindu and Buddhist philosophical and religious tradition. Mahayogi Guru Gorakhnath, who is the early Guru of the sect, is revered as one of the 84 *Maha Siddhas* in the Mahayana Buddhist tradition. He is known as *Goraksh* in the Tibetan Buddhist tradition. Hinduism and Buddhism, both, are integral to the oriental tradition of tolerance, which believes in listening to other points of view.

Ancient Indian philosophy lays emphasis on understanding the norms and thoughts processes of other religions, before reacting to them. Indian philosophy i.e. Hinduism, is not dogmatic in its approach nor antagonistic to the beliefs of others. Tolerance and respect for diverse spiritual philosophies has always underpinned the Indian way of life, from times immemorial. We believe in reconciliation, not recrimination. Our watch-word has always been consensus, not conflict. Even if the outlook of others is different from ours, we respect them no less for that. Aware as we are of the frailties of human nature, we do not thrust our point of view on others. We do not claim infallibility because we know, only the Almighty God is infallible.

Introspection and self-analysis are a way of life in Hinduism and this is how *Meemansa* and *Vivechana* are able to replace *Dvanda* i.e. strife and doubt. Four sequential steps have been prescribed to attain mental equilibrium in order to remove *Dvanda*. Of these, the first step is *Shravan* i.e. 'listening' ; the second step is *Manana* i.e. contemplation ; the third is *Chintana* i.e. meditation and the fourth is *keertan* i.e. giving vocal expression to one's feelings and emotions.

There are many instances in our tradition where discussion and exchange of thoughts is preferred to imposing a point of view by force. As is widely known, the great Adi Shankaracharya, who was the first one to propound of *Advait Darshan*, while criss-crossing the length and breadth of India, happened to visit Varanasi, the eternal city on the banks of the holy Ganga in Uttar Pradesh. Here he engaged in a *Shashtrarth* i.e. intecllectual discussion with Mandan Misra, a renowned scholar, and follower of Poorva Mimansa thought. It is said that the *Shastrartha* continued for months together, without rancour.

We have inherited this glorious tradition of tolerance and peaceful accommodation of ideas, that differ from our own—something which has almost vanished in the contemporary world. Peaceful discussion in an amicable environment should alone be the guiding principle for resolving differences so that society, and indeed, mankind is saved from decimation and ultimate annihilation.

In the *Mahabharata,* Lord Krishna did his best to negotiate with the Kauravas even though there was no power which he did not possess. He could have prevailed upon the Kauravas, but he was in search of a peaceful solution. Krishna himself, went all the way to the court of Hastinapur as an ambassador of peace and mediator, on behalf of the Pandavas. Lord Krishna left no stone unturned to come to a peaceful settlement with the Kaurvas, which unhappily, was not to be. The sum and substance of it all is that even God Almighty preferred peace to a contest. Lord Buddha was no different from Krishna in so far as peace and harmony were a concerned. He was a great exponent of peace, saying 'no' to confrontation of any kind. He propagated and believed that 'victory over one's own self is better than victory in a thousand wars.' And this old message has continued to be the bedrock of our national and International policies.

Today we see strife and confrontation throughout the world, over almost all issues even those that are essential to human survival, as for instance the conversation on environment. It is a matter of utmost importance and brooks no delay. The alternative to it is perdition.

Conservation of the environment and sustainable development are a massive challenge and must be faced squarely because they are a matter of life and death for all of us. The environment includes everything—atmosphere, water, air, earth, vegetation, fauna, without which human life would be impossible to contemplate.

It is time to revive the teachings of Lord Buddha and his concept of *Dhamma* if the world has to progress towards peace and prosperity. We must pay close attention and respect to, what is called the *Astanga Marga*, of which *Samyak Dristi* and *Samyak Sankalpa,* are the foremost. We can find solutions to all our problems, from confrontation to environmental conservation by following the teachings of the Tathagata. From one perspective, all nature is inter-dependent we human beings, have to play a significant role to ensure that these components are balanced, and herein enters religion, which is vital for sensitising human beings to think and act better. Scriptures show us the path of righteousness, which unfortunately the contemporary generation finds too difficult to accommodate because it is caught up in the enjoyment of mundane pleasures. Believe it or not, this directly affects us and our environment.

Given this state of affairs, responsible institutions in the world will have to come forward to build mutual co-operation and goodwill, for preserving a sustainable environment. If humanity and the entire human civilisation are not to disappear from the face of the earth, no time should be lost to hark back to our mentors and God like saints like the great Buddha. It must, however, be said that this is an initiative, which cannot be left to the governments of the world alone. Every single human being, irrespective of nationality, religion, caste, profession or status must to his fullest ability strive to make this earth of ours, a truly habitable planet which will endure for millenniums to come. It is well within our hands, whether high or low, big or small, powerful or not so powerful to contribute to the emergence of a social order, where the greatest good would be easily available to the greater number.

This truth was grasped by Lord Buddha, thousands of years ago. *Abhidhammapitak* in Buddhism and *Khaddarshan* in the Hindu religion believe in the birth of form from the formless, from the abstract to concrete. This has been the most significant and fundamental spiritual event in the process of the creation of the universe, which further shows that we, living beings, are born from a common source of energy. This leaves no scope for any confusion or diversity. From this perspective, we are also naturally connected with our surrounding environment.

The first sermon of Lord Buddha to his five disciples begins by asking them to follow the golden middle path, that is the *Madhyam Padamarg* that will ensure balanced judgment and the sustainable conservation of environment.

Having realised the Truth himself, Lord Buddha wanted to share it with the masses. He knew that it was a difficult task, entailing suffering but overflowing, as he was with love and kindness for humanity at large, he opted for a life of absolute renunciation and asceticism to disseminate his message himself, and through his band of dedicated disciples.

We have inherited the legacy of Lord Rama, Lord Krishna and Lord Buddha, which is reflected in the activities of the government of Uttar Pradesh, that is committed to the welfare of one and all, by pursuing the path of "Sabka Saath, Sabka Vikas". The state government is also developing a Ramayana Circuit, a Krishna Circuit and a Buddhist Circuit so that their messages can be imbibed by everyone, including tourists from abroad. A little less than two years from now in 2019, we shall celebrate the *Ardha Kumbha* at holy *Prayag*—modern day Allahabad, where millions of pilgrims will converge both from within the country and abroad. As a spiritual and religious event, it is going to be quite a spectacle, the biggest human congregation of its kind. It is something to be seen to believed and I take this opportunity to invite you all most cordially, to visit the Kumbh and tour the state of Uttar Pradesh, which has always had a reputation for showing warmth and hospitality towards guests. It will be the pleasure of my government as, indeed my own to welcome you to the state.

I would also like to place on record my special thanks to the Most Venerable Abhidhajja Maharatha Guru Dr Ashin Nyanssara Ji, who is globally renowned as Sitagu Sayadaw. He is a great preacher and Dharma Guru, who preaches universal recognition and respect for welfare for all, without discrimination of any kind.

He is a well wisher and friend of India and its people and it is my privilege to congratulate him on having organised such a splendid and meaningful convention, dedicated to the welfare of the citizens of the world.

I extend my cordial thanks to one and all for gracing the occasion, and making it a success.

My special thanks to the organising Committee of Sitagu International Buddhist Academy, Myanmar Institute of International and Strategic Studies, Myanmar Institute of International and Strategic Studies and the Vivekananda International Foundation.

I also extend my heartfelt thanks to the government of Myanmar and its various ministries and departments for their valuable contribution to this international meet. I would like to conclude my speech by invoking an ancient Hindu mantra which seeks peace, harmony, health and happiness for all sentient beings.

ॐ सर्वे भवन्तु सुखिनः
सर्वे सन्तु निरामयाः ।
सर्वे भद्राणि पश्यन्तु
मा- कश्चिद्दुः खभाग्भवेत् ।
ॐ शान्तिः शान्तिः शान्तिः ॥

It means:

Om,
May All be Happy,
May All be Healthy (Free from Illness)
May All See what is Auspicious,
May no one Suffer in any way.
Om Peace, Peace, Peace.

(Mahant Yogi Adityanath is the Chief Minister of Uttar Pradesh, India)

5

Vote of Thanks: NC Vij

IT is a privilege and a matter of great joy for me to extend a vote of thanks to all those who have contributed in one way or the other to make Samvad–II: Dialogue for Peace, Harmony and Security a great success.

I must stress that the success of this edition of Samvad owes a lot to the personal indulgence of Most Venerable Sitagu Sayadaw Dr Ashin Nyanisara and his incredible team at Sitagu International Buddhist Academy, Yangon. On behalf of VIF I wish to express my gratitude and sincere thanks to Sitagu Sayadaw, the faculty, staff, students and the volunteers who have worked extremely hard, both in the foreground and background. You all deserve congratulations for a job well done and a huge round of applause.

Contribution of Myanmar Institute of Strategic and International Studies has also been immense and sincere thanks to the Chairman, Ambassador U Nyunt Maung Shein and his wonderful team at MISIS for their wholehearted cooperation. On this occasion, I also wish to thank the Ministry of Foreign Affairs, and all the other ministries and departments of Govt of Myanmar who have contributed to the successful organisation of this edition of Samvad and our comfortable stay.

A big thanks to our partners Japan Foundation and the embassy of Japan in Yangon and New Delhi for their unstinted support and participation in this edition of Samvad.

The success of any conference is always dependent on the intelligent and intellectual inputs of the participants as was the case in this particular conclave. We express our gratefulness to the most Venerable spiritual masters of six major faiths of the word Hinduism, Buddhism, Christianity, Islam, Sikhism and Jainism for blessing us by their gracious presence. You have guided us in the right direction by sharing your collective wisdom and we all feel immensely blessed and motivated.

The galaxy of learned scholars from various countries have brought here with them their knowledge and experiences. We would like to acknowledge our esteemed speakers and other delegates who took time out of their busy schedule and showered us with their pearls of wisdom and knowledge. We are truly humbled by your presence. Thank you for your invaluable contribution.

Ladies and Gentlemen, the Prime Ministers of India and Japan have been the driving force behind Samvad initiative. I wish to join all of you in thanking them for inspiring us with their remarkable video messages.

Before concluding, let me express our sincere gratitude to the Honourable Ministers from Myanmar, Sri Lanka and India and our Chief Guests, His Excellency the Governor of Uttar Pradesh Shri Ram Naik, the Honourable Chief Minister Mahant Yogi Adityanath, the Chief Minister of Yangon region Mr U Phyo Min Thien and His Excellency the National Security Advisor of Myanmar Mr U Thaung Tun for your participation and thoughtful address. You have graced this occasion with your presence.

We would also like to convey our deepest appreciation and convey our gratitude to the team of scholars led by Shri Gurumurthy from India, who conceived and constructed the entire concept of this conclave and laid down the intellectual roadmap for this conference. A word of thanks for unstinting support and hard work by my colleagues in VIF without who we could not have managed to hold this conclave. The list is too long to mention their names, but allow me to mention three, Anuttama Ganguly, Mr. Amitabh Mathur, and Mr Ashok Wangdi, who really have worked their guts out.

Furthermore, let's have a special recognition to the audience who remained patient throughout and encouraged the speakers by their gusto and enthusiasm. Thank you so much for being our pillars of support. Let's have a big round of applause for our lovely audience.

Last but not the least, I would also like to thank each and every one of you ladies and gentlemen, and wonderful and peace-loving people of Myanmar for your active and thoughtful participation.

(General NC Vij is Former Chief of Indian Army. He was Director VIF from 2014–2017)

YANGON DECLARATION

THE Interfaith Dialogue for Peace, Harmony and Security of the World, jointly organized by the Sitagu International Buddhist Missionary Association (SIBMA), Myanmar; the Vivekananda International Foundation (VIF), India; and the Myanmar Institute of Strategic and International Studies (Myanmar ISIS) in association with The Japan Foundation, Japan, was held at the Sitagu International Buddhist Academy (SIBA) on 5 and 6 August 2017 in Yangon. The Spiritual Masters of Buddhism, Christianity, Hinduism, Islam, Jainism, Sikh and more than 100 delegates from 30 countries participated in the Dialogue. Prime Minister H.E. Shri Narendra Modi of the Republic of India and Prime Minister H.E. Mr. Shinzo Abe of Japan sent their video messages to the inaugural session of the Dialogue. H.E. Thura U Aung Ko, Union Minister for Religious Affairs and Culture of the Government of Republic of the Union of Myanmar, H.E. U Thaung Tun, National Security Advisor of the Republic of the Union of Myanmar, H.E. Shri Ram Naik, Hon'ble Governor of Uttar Pradesh, India and H.E. Mr Nobuo Kishi, State Minister for Foreign Affairs of Japan delivered special addresses at the inaugural session. Hon'ble Chief Minister of Uttar Pradesh, India Mahant Yogi Adityanath delivered a valedictory address.

Spiritual/religious leaders of all religions, and scholars of all the religions actively participated in the discussion. We unanimously agree and declare on this Sixth of the Month of August, Two Thousand and Seventeenth that:

1. All the people of the world have to cooperate and endeavour together, without any fear, in order to obtain harmonious social life with full security assurances.
2. We denounce all kinds of hate speech, false propaganda, conflict and war under the pretext of religion and strongly condemn those who provide support any such activities.
3. We, leaders of all religions of the world, resolve to be builders of the harmonious human society by religious teachings and involve ourselves in consolidating peace and security of the world.
4. We, members of different faiths, need to build mutual understanding, respect and trust among ourselves in order to obtain a peaceful, secure and prosperous human society.
5. We resolve to exercise restraint and refrain from interfering in matters of other religions and to cooperate in building bridges for world peace.
6. It is our inherent duty to conserve the environment before it is too late for the survival of humankind.
7. All religious leaders from India present at this Samvad II have unanimously decided to meet once in every four months (and as and when it is required), starting from 4 December 2017 to build bridges and harmony.
8. We shall collectively initiate programmes to enhance environmental consciousness and undertake awareness/ protection projects.
9. To strengthen understanding and trust, we shall organize an interfaith camp for meditation.
10. All the spiritual paths and religious traditions are equally valid.

Index